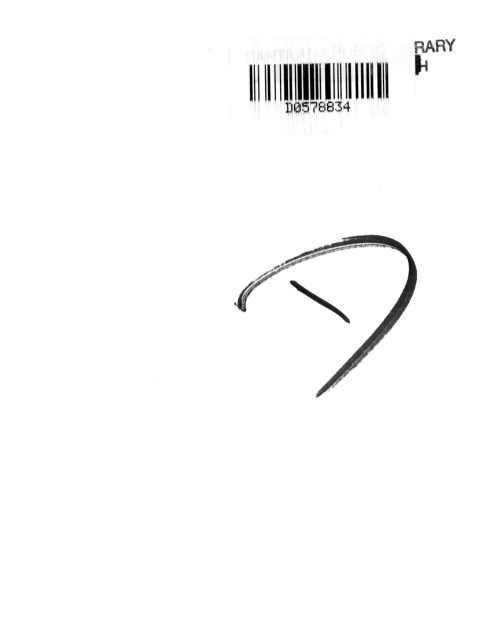

Crewel
Embroidery
in England

Crewel
Embroidery
in England

Joan Edwards

William Morrow & Company, Inc.

New York

Produced by Walter Parrish International Limited, London

Designed by Judy A. Tuke

Printed and bound in Spain by Roner SA, Madrid
Dep. Legal: SS. 133-1975

Library of Congress Catalog Card Number 74-29088

ISBN 0-688-02919-1

for Muriel Bredin and Dorothy Edwards

Young girl at her embroidery frame by Louisa, Marchioness of Waterford, c. 1865.

Author's acknowledgements

Into this book has gone the results of fairly wide reading, undertaken more often than not because a student has asked a question the answer to which I did not know, or because a group of embroiderers has invited me to give a lecture on a subject that has made me think about embroidery in a different way. So to all the embroiderers I have taught, in America as well as in England, I find myself more deeply indebted than they will ever be to me.

Next I must thank Mrs Madeleine Mainstone, Keeper of the Education Department in the Victoria and Albert Museum, for giving me the opportunity to work in the museum in a teaching as distinct from a curatorial situation, and for encouraging me to plan courses in which the practice of embroidery ceases to be an end in itself and becomes a central pivot from which the embroiderer can set out to explore the other decorative arts, and to find beyond them the great fine arts, and beyond them again history, geography, and the trade routes of the world along which embroideries and embroidery patterns have been travelling since before history was ever written down.

To the rest of the staff of the Department I offer my grateful thanks for much help and many memorable kindnesses, as well as to Mr Donald King, Keeper of Textiles, Mrs Barbara Morris, Circulation Department, Miss Betty Tyres, India Department, and Miss Norah Gillow of the William Morris Gallery.

I have also good reason to thank my friend Mrs Dorothea Nield—embroiderer, teacher, author, and former Head Teacher in the Royal School of Needlework's training school—for working the stitch samplers; Mrs Betty Buddle for generously allowing me to use her material on Abigail Pett; and Mrs Pauline Dower for making available to me the notes made by her mother, Lady Mary Trevelyan, on her crewel work panel.

At Walter Parrish International, who produced the book, I must thank Mrs Phoebe Phillips who has master-minded the whole enterprise with enthusiasm and encouraging words spoken at exactly the right moment; Mrs Jane Maitland Hudson who collected the illustrations; Mr Trevor Vertigan who made the line drawings; and other helpful members of the staff each of whom has contributed their particular skill to the making of this book. With them I would like to include Mrs Virginia Goldie for her assistance with typing the manuscript.

To the affectionate conviction of my cousin, Joy Lee, that I could do what has often seemed impossible and actually write a book on crewel work, and to the critical attention with which on innumerable occasions she has patiently submitted to having the text read aloud to her, I owe more than words can tell.

Joan Edwards
London 1975

Contents

Colour illustrations

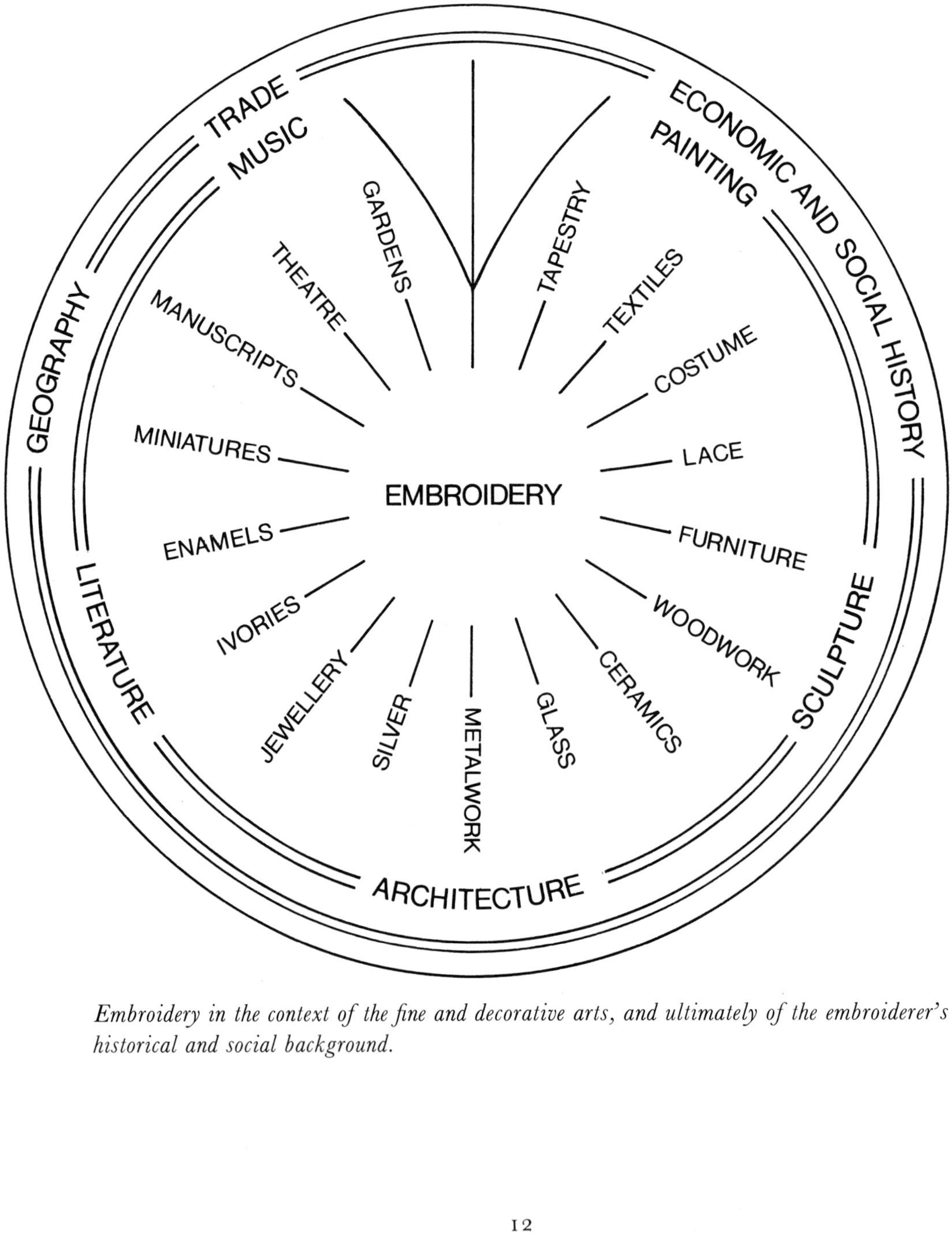
TRADE
ECONOMIC AND SOCIAL HISTORY
GEOGRAPHY
LITERATURE
ARCHITECTURE
SCULPTURE
MUSIC
PAINTING
GARDENS
TAPESTRY
THEATRE
TEXTILES
MANUSCRIPTS
COSTUME
MINIATURES
LACE
EMBROIDERY
ENAMELS
FURNITURE
IVORIES
WOODWORK
JEWELLERY
CERAMICS
SILVER
GLASS
METALWORK

Embroidery in the context of the fine and decorative arts, and ultimately of the embroiderer's historical and social background.

Prologue

To the Gentle Reader:
    As I have (with my no little travayle)
collected this History . . . so most gentle
and loving Reader, I beseche thee take these
my travayles not only in good part, but also
pardon the rudenesse of my stile and lacke
of learning which I acknowledge, or otherwise
the same should have been better furnished.

Richard Grafton, 1569

As far as I know nobody has ever previously attempted to give an account of the various ways in which the English embroiderer has used her crewel wools. So in writing this book I have allowed my thoughts about them to develop by association, letting each part dissolve into the next like the scenes in a play in which the embroiderer herself is the leading lady.

Here we see her using her crewels on the Bayeux Tapestry for couching and laid work; there for canvas work and needle painting; and in the workrooms of Morris & Company and the Royal School of Needlework for enormous hangings densely covered with long and short stitch.

But it was the seventeenth century embroiderer who, taking one glance at the patterns on the painted cotton hangings imported from India by the directors of the East India Company, suddenly pushed aside the tiny inhabitants of her stumpwork world, the minute stitchery of her mirror frames, pictures, and caskets, and with tremendous vigour, zest, and excitement, created out of one of the commonest and coarsest of household textiles and her crewel wools an entirely new method of embroidery that we today call crewel work. It was one of the great moments in the history of embroidery.

All the king's horses
and all the king's men

By the needle thou shalt draw the
thread and by that which is past see
how that which is to come will be drawn.

George Herbert, 1640

On 29 November 1803, a French newspaper announced that an important
historical document of a most unusual kind—*La Tapisserie de la Reine Matilde*—
had arrived in Paris from the small market town of Bayeux and was to be exhibited at the Musée Napoléon.

The occasion was not without a certain piquancy. It was only fourteen years
since the French Revolution. In this brief period Napoleon had made himself
master of a large part of Western Europe. Inevitably his plans included a large
scale invasion of England and already troops and transports were being assembled
on the coast of Normandy.

Napoleon visited the exhibition and studied the Tapestry thoughtfully.
What significance, if any, did he attach to the appearance in the French capital
at this particular moment of the miraculously preserved embroidery, worked
in crewel wools, on which was spelt out the story of the successful conquest of
England by a Norman French duke in 1066? It was noticed that he paid particular
attention to the incident of the fiery comet that plainly struck such awe into the
hearts of those who observed it. He saw the newly crowned King Harold tremble,
and the ghostly hulls of the French ships that he feared soon to see approaching
the shores of his kingdom. What signs and portents Napoleon read into the tale
we shall never know. It is not without interest however, that in the summer of
1941, when Hitler was preparing to invade England, four art experts should have
been sent to study the Tapestry and make copies of it.

1 Stothard's drawing of the damage at the beginning of the Tapestry. The embroidery was subsequently restored.

The exhibition at the Musée Napoléon enjoyed an enormous popular success. A one-act play was quickly written and put on at the Théâtre du Vaudeville based upon the story of the Norman Conquest. In it Queen Matilde was seen working busily at her embroidery while awaiting the return of her lord from battle.

But in England rumours of the intended invasion by the French were rife and the English embroiderers correspondingly fearful. One of them, Miss Catherine Hutton, who lived not far from Birmingham, laid aside her needle to comment on the situation. The mother of her friend might forbid her daughter to visit Miss Hutton, 'as she durst not let her go from home for fear of Bonaparte's threatened invasion', but she herself was made of sterner stuff.

> I do not believe [she wrote loftily] that Bonaparte eats men and women, nor do I believe that he ransacks their graves for their bones. Though an arrant coward by nature on common occasions, I have always found courage for great ones.

However there were to be no calls upon her valour. Napoleon changed his plans and the Tapestry was rolled up and returned to the authorities at Bayeux who, to give them their due, had parted with their treasure with the greatest misgivings. It came back accompanied by a letter from the director of the Musée Napoléon. He wrote

> I am returning to you the Tapestry embroidered by La Reine Matilde. The First Consul was much pleased to see this relic of our history. He admired the care with which the citizens of Bayeux have preserved it through the centuries. He has instructed me to express to them his complete satisfaction, and to entrust it once again to their safekeeping.

The citizens have done their work well. In 1945 they created a permanent gallery for it in the old bishop's palace, a modest eighteenth century château with tall windows, a pleasant garden, and a broad lawn with shady trees. On the opposite side of the steep paved street stands the cathedral with which the Tapestry has for so long been associated. It was already there when, in 1472, an inventory of its treasures was taken. It was described as

> A very long and very narrow strip or hanging embroidered with figures and inscriptions representing the Norman conquest of England, which is hung round the church on the Feast of Relics and throughout the octave.

Plainly in the fifteenth century there was no confusion in men's minds between embroidery and tapestry.

Then for nearly two hundred and fifty years there is silence.

The eighteenth century gentleman prided himself upon being a man of taste and erudition: a scholar, bibliophile, connoisseur, and antiquarian. His interests included art, architecture, music, literature, and gardening. He collected paintings and sculpture, portfolios of drawings of ancient monuments, medals, coins, and ceramics. In so far as his purse permitted he was a traveller, particularly in France and Italy. As a fellow of one or other of the learned societies dedicated

2 Harold with a hawk on his wrist and preceded by his hounds rides to Bosham.

to the publication of original research and to financing archaeological expeditions, he read papers at their meetings and played an active part in the subsequent discussions. If he was a Frenchman he probably belonged to the *Académie Royale des Inscriptions et Belles-Lettres*.

On 21 July 1724, this organisation received a paper from one of its most distinguished members, Monsieur Lancelot. His subject was a neatly executed drawing of a curious object which had been sent to him for identification. Unable to decide from the sketch whether it was a narrative bas-relief from a tomb or stained glass window, a fresco, or a tapestry, he placed the matter before the members in a communication entitled *Explication d'un monument de Guillaume le Conquérant*.

As the sketch had come originally from a collection formed by a learned gentleman named Foucault who lived in Normandy, it seemed only reasonable to suppose that the interesting object might be located in that area. Lancelot, however, received no reply to the letters he addressed to the authorities at Caen, the principal town in the district. Hearing of his dilemma, a Benedictine monk, Dom Bernard de Montfaucon, took up the case and began to make inquiries through the monasteries at Caen and Bayeux. He soon discovered that the sketch was of the first part of an ancient piece of embroidery in the cathedral at Bayeux and, in 1729, he published it in his study of the *Monuments de la Monarchie française*. Later he sent a draughtsman to copy the rest of the design and this he also published with an admirable essay.

Some years later an archaeologist named Ducarel, made a tour of Normandy with the object of studying its antiquities. He visited Bayeux and asked to see what he described rather loosely as 'a long strip of linen having some connection with William the Conqueror'. Nobody seemed to be very clear exactly what they were being asked to produce. Eventually it dawned upon them that the eccentric Englishman must be referring to the *Tapisserie* they hung round the nave on the Feast of Relics, and which was kept during the rest of the year in the chapel dedicated to St Thomas of Canterbury.

Then came the French Revolution. The Tapestry was twice saved in the nick of time from destruction: once through the spirited oratory of a local lawyer who persuaded some new recruits, filled with republican zeal, to abandon their scheme for using it as packing for their waggons; and again when, through the timely intervention of the town councillors, some over-enthusiastic citizens were prevented from tearing it up to make bunting for a float they were decorating to take part in a procession on a public holiday.

In 1818 the Society of Antiquaries of London despatched an experienced and conscientious draughtsman, Charles Stothard, to Bayeux with instructions to make an exact copy of the Tapestry in colour. His drawings were published by the Society in 1819.

Upon comparing the drawings of his predecessors with the Tapestry, Stothard was dismayed to find how rapidly its condition had deteriorated. Near the beginning, part of the scene in which Harold rides to Bosham had been torn away and the edges roughly cobbled together. He carefully unpicked the crude stitches and straightened the figures [1].

3 An incident in the Battle of Hastings.

In other parts, where the wools had disappeared altogether, he found that he could reconstruct the design from the tiny needle pricks left behind on the linen. On examining some of these he noticed that minute particles of wool still adhered to them, and thus discovered what colours the embroider had used. In his report, he suggested that with this information it should be possible to restore some of the stitchery, pointing out that if the work was not quickly put in hand it would be too late. This may well be the first occasion on which the idea of conserving a piece of old and valuable embroidery was ever seriously proposed.

Like all crewel work the stitchery is definite, decisive, surprisingly quick, and very economical. The linen, the worsted spun wools, and the honest, straight-forward method employed by the embroiderers perfectly expressed the spirited design. Like the men who meet, plot, feast, and fight their way round a strip of material that was originally rather more than 230 yards long and some 20 inches wide, the needlework is vigorous, outspoken, and colloquial. It has none of the refinements of the disciplined technique, the silks and the gold threads so appropriate for executing the calm, withdrawn little saints on the stole and maniple ordered by Edward the Elder's Queen Aelfflaeda a hundred and fifty years earlier as a gift for the bishop of Winchester. These strong feudal overlords—Harold, William, Bishop Odo—and the English and French soldiers hacking each other to pieces called for stronger, rougher treatment. Like the embroiderers themselves, they were contemporary men, caught up in the tide of contemporary events. So the Bayeux Tapestry is 'contemporary' embroidery of a particularly notable kind.

As with all embroidery, the Tapestery is best seen at eye level, and on this count alone it may be questioned whether Bishop Odo, William's half-brother, who it is generally agreed commissioned it, ever intended to hang it in his cathedral. Furthermore, if it was to be viewed on high days and holidays by the good citizens of Bayeux, it is surely curious that their bishop should have allowed himself to be presented to them as a warrior baron rather than as a great ecclesiastical dignitary. It would not have taken them long to discover that apart from his tonsure and vestments, he appears throughout the story as a man of violent action rather than as a peaceful servant of God; and that where they might justifiably have expected to see him—that is, in the important scene on which the whole story turns, when Harold makes his solemn oath of loyalty to William, swearing on sacred relics resting on two altars—he is nowhere to be found. But when the decision to invade England is taken, and the building of the ships to transport the troops put in hand, Odo is at William's side sharing in the plans and issuing orders with wide, emphatic gestures. Again he is at William's right hand when a council of war is held after the landing at Pevensey, and once the battle is joined he is in the thick of the fight, spurring on the younger soldiers. Indeed his only religious act in the entire story is the purely formal one of saying grace. It was Harold who, before embarking upon his journey to France, stops to pray in Bosham church; but it was Odo who, as William's vice-regent, enriched himself at the expense of the English churches, and built himself palaces that were known for their lavishness of decoration and filled with sump-tuous and beautiful objects. Did he perhaps commission the Tapestry for one of them, or maybe as a commemorative gift to Queen Matilda? The fact that the wedding clothes worn by William and Matilda appear in the inventory of 1472 together with the Tapestry, suggests that it must have been at some time in the castle at Bayeux.

Although references to it are not easily found, it must be assumed that by the end of the eleventh century there was a well-established tradition of narrative embroidery in south east England. There was certainly a notable school of manuscript illumination at Canterbury, and it may well have been to these artists that Odo entrusted the task of designing his Tapestry.

But at some point there had to be a writer—a man capable of composing the slender, lively chronicle that endows each scene with its special immediacy. By his skilful use of the tiny latin word *hic*, that is, *here*, he draws the spectator into the story and involves him in each event as it comes round. He wrote

here   Harold sailed the sea and with the wind full in his sails he came to the country of Count Guy.

here   Guy seizes Harold.

here   Guy brought Harold to William Duke of the Normans.

here   Duke William comes with Harold to his palace.

here   Duke William and his army came to Mont Saint-Michel and *here* they crossed the river Couesnon.

here   William gives arms to Harold.

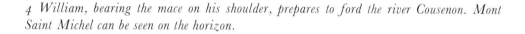

4 William, bearing the mace on his shoulder, prepares to ford the river Cousenon. Mont Saint Michel can be seen on the horizon.

<table>
<tr><td>here</td><td>Duke Harold returned to English soil and came to King Edward.</td></tr>
<tr><td>here</td><td>is the body of King Edward carried to the church of St Peter the Apostle.</td></tr>
<tr><td>here</td><td>they have given the crown to Harold.</td></tr>
<tr><td>here</td><td>Duke William in a great ship crossed the sea and came to Pevensey.</td></tr>
<tr><td>here</td><td>the soldiers went out of Hastings and came to the battle against King Harold.</td></tr>
<tr><td>here</td><td>the English and French fell together in battle. And finally,</td></tr>
<tr><td>here</td><td>King Harold has been killed and the English have turned in flight.</td></tr>
</table>

Given the narrative, plans for illustrating it could be put in hand. It is considered likely that a group of artists rather than one man was engaged in composing the design. Presumably their terms of reference included such information as how long it was to be and how wide. The intention to enclose the story in four borders was almost certainly part of the original scheme, if only because they are so essential to its overall effect. They contain, unite, and stabilise it. They are not only highly decorative and abounding in interesting details, but their very smallness tricks our eye into believing that the figures taking part in the narrative are larger than is actually the case. Diagonal lines divide them into

5 As the ships cast anchor on the French coast, Harold is met and seized by Count Guy, a vassal of Duke William.

compartments of various sizes inhabited by a miscellaneous assortment of birds, monsters, fables, enchanting little agricultural scenes and foliage. Towards the end, the lower border serves not only as a shelter from which bowmen can take aim but also as a ditch or common grave into which fall the dismembered bodies of the men and horses slain in the battle.

A more subtle device than the diagonal lines had to be found to indicate to the viewers, who could not necessarily read the narrative itself, that one incident in the long, helter-skelter story was over and another about to begin. The choice fell on trees with interlacing branches conveniently twining in two directions at once, and free-standing towers, all of them old ideas borrowed by early medieval artists from the paintings of classical antiquity. But occasionally the designers dispensed with these landmarks and contained a scene within a building, introducing a quite astonishing sense of space and size into the design by allowing the top of the roof and its pinnacles to escape into the upper border; while by means of a pointing finger and a head turned away from the scene in which a character is participating, a break in continuity is often clearly indicated.

The design itself is completely flat and devoid of perspective. It is taken for granted that the spectator is familiar with the convention that if something is far away it will be placed high up in the picture: hence the position of Mont Saint-Michel in the scene in which William and his troops ford the river Couesnon on their way to attack the Castle of Dol in Brittany. The men, horses, ships, buildings, and trees are all about the same size: but how much urgent activity

is conveyed to us by the lively manner in which they are grouped. At one moment they are crowded together in a densely packed bunch, and at the next have moved away from each other, spreading out across the linen. Before long the spaces between them are closing up and soon another tight, terse group begins to form. This in turn breaks up, disperses, and the process starts all over again. It is an essentially rhythmic movement; a device calculated to fix the spectator's attention, whet his curiosity, and encourage him to pursue the long epic drama to the bitter end.

Through the centuries a story has persisted that at the Battle of Hastings the French troops, led by William's minstrel, Taillefer, advanced against the English singing the great epic poems, or *chansons de geste*, about Charlemagne, the Frankish king who became master of the Holy Roman Empire, and Roland, his warrior nephew who, having been betrayed, died in battle against the Moors. As he rode, Taillefer twirled his sword about his head, tossed it high in the air, and caught it again. True or false the story recorded on the Tapestry has all the essential ingredients of a *chanson de geste*: a pitched battle between men of heroic stature in which the attackers seek to avenge some act of treachery committed against one of their number by the attacked. So although the message of the story is angled strongly in support of the French view of the events, it was as readily understood by the spectator as any of the other conventions, tricks, and devices hidden in it.

Harold was a strong man. It was he, not William, who rescued the soldiers from the quicksands of the Couesnon. He was no coward, no laggard in war. His weaknesses were moral rather than physical and he was twice a convicted traitor. In so far as he knew it to be Edward's wish that William should succeed him—and was in fact the intermediary between them—in taking the crown he betrayed his king. In accepting arms from William and swearing a double oath of fealty to him, even if, as the pointing fingers of William and his vassals seem to indicate, he did so under duress, he broke every rule of chivalry by betraying his feudal overlord. In that this man had also been his friend and had delivered him from the hands of his enemy, Count Guy, Harold's conduct is made to appear even more infamous and the retribution, at least in Norman eyes, completely justified.

And what of the embroiderers themselves, these early masters of crewel work, whose business it was to interpret this magnificent design? The methods they employed—laid work and couching—are typical gold work techniques, and it is reasonably certain that in the medieval professional workrooms, gold work was generally done by men. Taken in conjunction with the extreme harshness of the crewel wools, which are better suited to men's than women's fingers, it seems likely that both men and women worked on the Tapestry. But who knows? Two things only are reasonably certain: that the needles had large eyes, and that because laid work and couching cannot be satisfactorily performed in the hand, the Tapestry was in all probability worked on a frame.

An embroidery frame is made of four pieces of wood: usually two short rollers and a pair of long flat side pieces. One end of the textile is attached to a roller and wound smoothly onto it. A short strip is then unwound and attached to the other roller. How much of the design is exposed between the rollers depends upon the number of embroiderers who can sit comfortably around it—perhaps four on each long side. After lashing the side pieces to the rollers, the edges of the textiles are laced to them and the frame is supported at either end on trestles. By adjusting the rollers and laces the textile is pulled taut and straight. As each part of the design is finished the laces are removed and the textile is rolled on, drawing out in its wake the next unworked section. The laces are then replaced, the tension adjusted, and the work begins all over again.

The design of the Bayeux Tapestry was not transferred to a single continuous strip of linen but onto several pieces of different length. It is likely that each piece was framed up separately, thus increasing the number of embroiderers who could work on it simultaneously, thereby reducing the time taken to complete it.

6 While men gaze in terror at the fiery comet, a courtier informs the newly crowned Harold of its appearance. Does it, he wonders, presage the imminent arrival of ships bearing William to take vengeance upon him?

Day after day these anonymous embroiderers worked at their task. Quickly and dexterously the wool was brought to the surface of the work at an appropriate point on the outline of the design, and carried straight across to the other side. Here the needle was thrust down through the linen, received below the frame by the left hand, and returned to the surface *immediately beside the place through which it had a moment before descended*. Once again it was carried across the design; thrust down next to the point from which it had first emerged; brought to the surface again; and carried back to the opposite side.

Backwards and forwards went the needle and thread across each part of the pattern until it was entirely covered with closely packed, long, straight stitches. These were then fixed firmly in place by means of a single matching thread laid across them at regular intervals, and secured with small, neat couching stitches. As a result of using this technique an enormous saving of wool was effected, the

7 William, with Bishop Odo seated beside him, plans the invasion of England.

maximum amount being left on the right side of the work and only the bare minimum on the wrong.

But in the hands of master craftsmen, whether men or women, embroidery becomes more than a simple exercise in filling in a pattern with stitchery. While in no sense attempting to copy exactly the nuances of the designer's pen, pencil, or brush, they are well qualified to transpose something of its essence into terms of needlework. So on top of the laid work and couching the embroiderers 'drew' long quick-moving lines of stem or outline stitch which, although in many ways a dull commonplace stitch, is extremely mobile and responsive to the slightest turning of the needle and thread. Every embroiderer knows that it is not so much the complexity of the stitch that is important as the skill and imagination with which it is used. From the workroom manager's point of view, however, the fact that outline stitch is rapidly worked must have greatly added to its usefulness.

Presumably the placing of the colours, if not the original choice, lay with the embroiderers. So various are the ways in which they have combined them that it is difficult to believe they had only eight at their disposal—the familiar pinkish terracotta, buff, yellow, two blues, and three greens. Such changes in tone as can be seen today are probably due to variability in the original dyes, to fading, and to subsequent restoration.

Three further points are perhaps worth noting. First, if the embroiderers sat on either side of the frame, one group would have had to work the design upside down. Second, when the outline stitch was being worked the embroiderers must from time to time have had to leave their places in order to consult the cartoon or full-scale drawing from which the design had been transferred, and which would almost certainly have been mounted somewhere in the workroom, in order to see exactly how such details as the folds of the drapery were to be put in, as the lines drawn on the linen by the artist would have been covered up by the laid work. Third, until each piece was finished, the laces removed for the last time, the linen unwound and out of the rollers, nobody knew just how successful or unsuccessful the final result of so much hard work would be.

Neither the design nor the execution has always earned unqualified praise. Montfaucon himself was of the opinion that the background as well as the design should have been covered with stitchery, while in 1888 another Frenchman, Ernest Léfebure, condemned the drawing of the figures as 'infantile'; and in 1884 Lady Mary Alford, one of the founders of the Royal School of Needlework, describes the style as 'childish', finding it in every way inferior to Queen Aelfflaeda's stole and maniple: 'they seem hardly to belong to the same period,' she wrote, 'so weak are the designs and the composition of the groups.'

But to our eyes it is the sheer virtuosity of the designers and the embroiderers that make the Tapestry notable. Any embroiderer who has made the journey to Bayeux and seen it stretching away into the distance against its pale buff background, has watched it turn across the end of the long gallery, return up the other side, and turn towards her again, knows suddenly that not even the most excellent drawing, or the best photographs succeed in catching its particular magic; and although the postcard which she carries away may serve for a time to jog her memory, in the end it serves only to weaken and diminish her experience. The Tapestry is great not simply because it is ancient, unique, priceless, and venerated; nor because it is an important historical document; but because it is eloquent, evocative, and beautiful. Because in its own right it is a work of art.

Entr'acte I

The use of sewing is extremely old,
As in the sacred text it is enrolled;
Our parents first in Paradise began
Who have descended since from man to man;
The mothers taught their daughters, sires their sons,
Thus in a line successively it runs
For general profit and for recreation,
From generation unto generation.

John Taylor, The Water Poet

Perhaps the greatest imponderable, the supreme enigma in the history of embroidery, is the embroiderer herself. Here is her work. One glance suffices to tell us that she was an able and accomplished needlewoman. That she was inventive, imaginative, clever at choosing the right stitch, and with a sure eye for a good colour scheme. But who is she? We may hazard a guess at when she lived, but even if she has signed her work, her name probably means nothing to us. Why did she make this valance? when did she wear this petticoat? on whose bed did she spread this coverlet? who taught her to do such beautiful embroidery? and why, when all the rest of her work has vanished, has this solitary example survived?

To see the embroiderer in the context of her own house and period is, except on rare occasions, denied us. Because we have no positive information about her, we tend to idealise her; to imagine—happy woman—that she had so much more time than we do to devote to embroidery; that she had fewer responsibilities, fewer interruptions and dutiful distractions. That wherever she was it was always summer time and therefore that she could sit all day, year in year out, in peaceful contentment in a garden full of flowers, where weeds never grew, or lawns and hedges needed to be trimmed, or fallen leaves swept up. With her frame in her hands, her daughters and friends gathered companionably around her, and innumerable servants waiting upon her, we enshrine her, as the artist does, in some magical earthly paradise [9].

But truth is often as strange and unexpected as fiction. The only way to get at the reality behind the dream is to read the books, poems, romances, plays, letters, and diaries contemporary with the embroidery, and therefore with the embroiderer herself. They paint a very different picture.

In his pamphlet on *The Education of Ladies,* Jonathan Swift confronts us with an embroiderer who is perpetually busy. As mistress of her husband's household and mother of his children, no day is ever long enough to accomplish all the duties she is expected to perform, and the possession of many servants only adds to her responsibilities. 'Her whole business,' he wrote, 'if well performed, will take up most hours of the day; and the more servants she keeps the greater will be her supervision.' Carried to its logical conclusion this means that although a lady may not be expected to carry out the more arduous household tasks herself, she must know the correct way of performing them, train her servants accordingly, and see that they maintain the high standard she sets them.

In a little book written in 1774 by Dr John Gregory, Professor of Medicine at Edinburgh University, the picture is brought into even sharper focus. Dr Gregory had lost his wife. Troubled over the fate of his motherless daughters, he wrote his letters for their comfort and guidance. We may believe that they express the opinions of the period, for new editions of the book were still coming out in 1828. 'The purpose of your being taught needlework, knitting, and such-like,' he told them, 'is not so much for the value of all you can do with your hands which is trifling, but to enable you to judge more perfectly of that kind of work, and direct its execution by others.'

It would be clearly wrong, therefore, to imagine that the average woman who, in the seventeenth and eighteenth centuries took up crewel work, had all the time in the world to devote to it. Embroidery was her relaxation.

The English at home

Like the Society of Antiquaries of London to whom we owe Stothard's drawings of the Bayeux Tapestry, local historical societies have always looked upon the publication of the accounts and inventories of prominent families connected with the area as one of their chief responsibilities. Understandably documents dealing with the affairs of royal and noble families have a better chance of survival than those of the landed gentry. Nevertheless it is in these more homely and intimate records that we find a pattern of daily living that relates more nearly to our own experience than the splendours of palaces and castles. They help us not only to visualise the embroiderer in her proper context but also to understand her embroidery better.

Between 1856 and 1858 the Cheetham Society of Manchester published an annotated version by John Harland, FSA, of the farm and household accounts of a well known Lancashire family, the Shuttleworths of Smithills and Gawthorpe. They cover the years 1582 to 1621. Because traditional patterns of household management changed very little up to the last century, we can take it that the picture they reflect is typical of the background against which the embroiderers of the second half of the seventeenth century, who were likely to be attracted to the new fashion for crewel work, lived out their steady lives. In them we see the family sheets, towels, blankets, and dishes being bought; their laundry sent out; their wives buried; and their daughters married. Even the tinker who received 2d (2 pence) for mending the dripping pan, and the waits who came regularly every Christmas are there, together with the half-yard of cloth purchased in 1610 for Lady Shuttleworth to rub her teeth, and the 2s (2 shillings) spent on 'stuffe to kill myce'.

The first mistress of Gawthorpe to appear in the accounts is Anne Grimshaw. She married Hugh Shuttleworth on 26 October 1540, and they had three sons and two daughters. The eldest son, Richard, became a judge at the Chester assizes; the second, Lawrence, took holy orders and became vicar of Whichford in Warwickshire; and the third son, Thomas, who predeceased his brothers but left a large family, seems to have devoted himself to managing the family estates. In due course, when his father died, Richard became head of the family, and

8 Detail of a repeating pattern on a seventeenth century bed curtain. The stems bear tulips, exotic flowers, and boldly decorative leaves.

Thomas acted as his steward and kept the farm and household accounts. In the beginning they deal chiefly with the maintenance of buildings and the payment of outdoor workers. James Norres was paid 7s 8d for 'a fatte calffe and a quere of paper'; a glazier received 7d for mending windows; Richard the smith had 7d for making staples to repair the lock on the barn door; and the man who made 'myttenes for the gardener' also earned 7d.

Drawings relating to illustration 8 (overleaf). A stitch key is given on page 222.

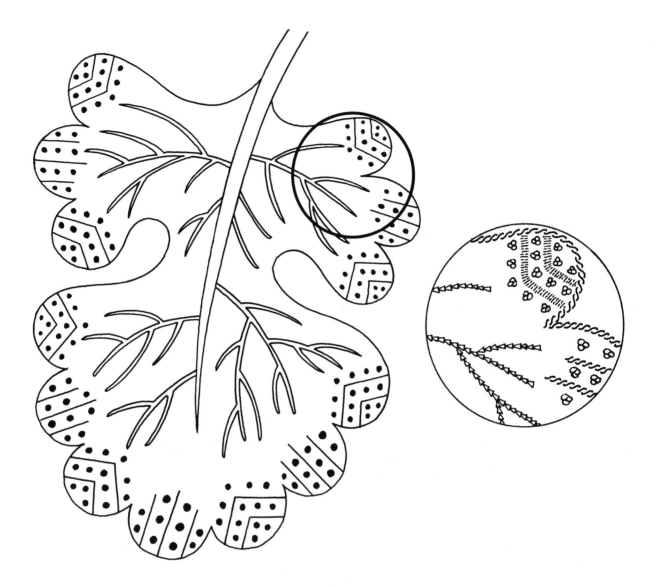

Then in April 1592 Lady Shuttleworth died. Apparently she had been in poor health for some time because in March 1591 she had been visited by Dr Coggan of Manchester, who charged 40s 'for his advice and the stuffe which he sent unto my Ladie'. At the same time six lemons were purchased for 9d presumably to make the 'sirripe of lemons' he prescribed for her. Suddenly in two terse entries we catch something of the shock of her death and the silence that followed it, broken by the sound of men riding through the night. Thomas Shuttleworth wrote: 'Given to Mr Boldre's mane, that did ride with Wm Kenion to Crostaffe in the night when my Ladie dyed, 12d'; and 'to Sir Richard Mullenex horse kep for ottes whene Wm Kenion went to Mr Peter Leighe, upon the death of my Ladie, 6d'. Subsequently he paid Thomas Marche 2s for making the coffin, 12d to the mason and his men who dug the grave, and 4d for a stone plate which presumably was to act as a temporary cover for it.

9 A group of noble ladies at work in a garden, c. 1634 from the album amicorum *of Gervasius Fabricus of Saltzburg.*

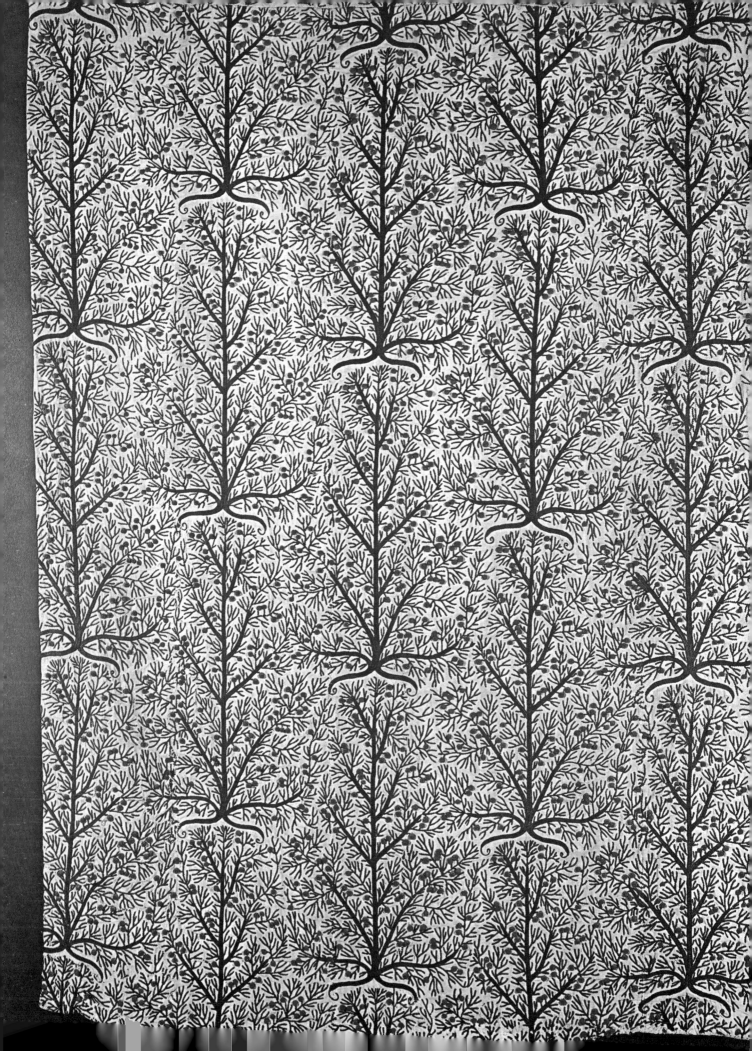

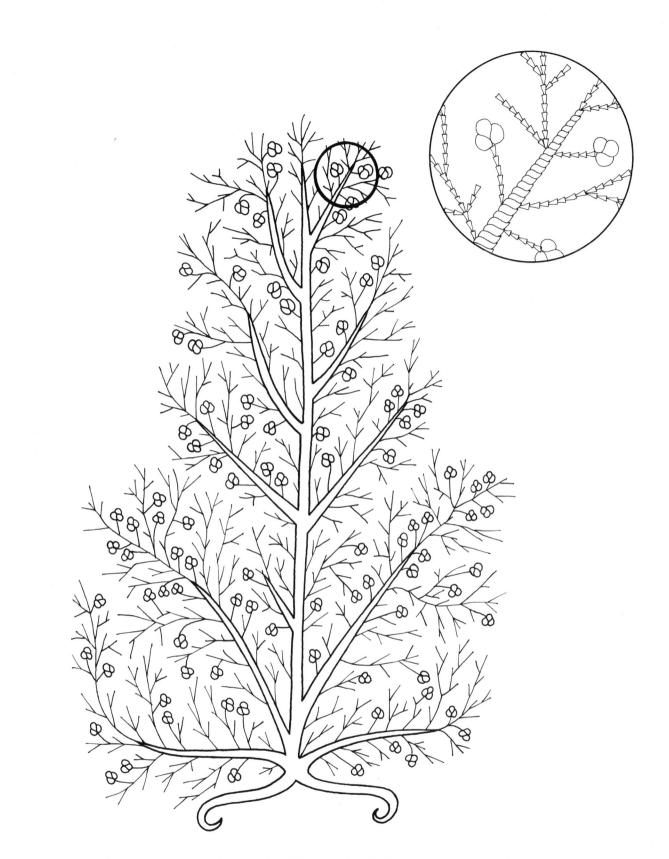

10 *Part of a seventeenth century bed curtain with conventionalised asparagus plants bearing red berries. The larger plants are approximately 18 inches high and the berries are worked in plaited knot (raised rose) stitch.*

Amid the solemn tolling of bells the coffin was carried on a litter drawn by two horses to Wynwicke church. The ringers received 5s, and those who rang at Bolton, Leigh and Deane churches had 3s 6d, 2s 6d, and 2s respectively. The priest was paid 3s 4d and his clerk 9d. Payment was also made for 44 yards of 'black cotten for the coverynge of the litter and barbing the two horses', and for 'a pounde of black thrid' to sew up the curtains. The tailors who made them charged 10s. Thomas also entered the cost of the food and drink provided at Wynwicke for the mourners. Eighteen of them dined at Richard Tailor's house and he received 58s 8d for their meal, plus 5s 5d for ale, and 8d for horse fodder, while 3s 4d was given to 'the wyffe of Wm Taliores the same daye for towe messe and half at dynner'. Finally, the customary dole was given to the poor; John Woodroffe presenting gifts amounting to 40s 7d 'unto the poore Folkes at Smithills', and Alexander Bradshawe 57s 4d to the poor at Wynwicke.

The next mistress of Gawthorpe was Richard Shuttleworth's wife. Perhaps by this time the old house at Gawthorpe had fallen into disrepair, because towards the end of the century plans were being made to replace it, the rebuilding co-inciding with the erection of Hardwick Hall in the neighbouring county of Derby-shire for the aged Countess of Shrewsbury. Although Gawthorpe was a much smaller house, it was built in exactly the same flat, angular style. The site chosen for it was on the banks of the river Calder not far from the village of Padiham. It was already occupied by an ancient square stone tower, and immediately opposite was a vast dark forest that swept up the slopes of Pendle Mountain crouching on the horizon, where witches were said to hold their orgies. Their story was told by W. Harrison Ainsworth in *The Witches of Pendle*. Reluctant perhaps to destroy an old landmark, the Shuttleworths decided to build their house around the old tower, which still stands out conspicuously above the roof. When the foundation stone was laid in the summer of 1600 the accounts show that money was given to the mason and his labourers, to the housekeeper and her maids, and to eight menservants—including the cow boy—to buy gloves.

Sir Richard and Lady Shuttleworth had no children and the estate passed to Lawrence who, while retaining his living at Whichford, lived at Gawthorpe and for a short time wrote up the accounts himself. Apparently he did not marry for when he died in 1607 he was succeeded by Thomas's eldest son, another Richard Shuttleworth, who had been born about 1587. He married Fleetwood, daughter and sole heir of Richard Barton of Rufford.

As a child, Fleetwood had been married to Richard, Lord Molyneux, but when he was fourteen he contracted out of the marriage and, as it had not been consummated, he was granted a divorce by the bishop of Chester. Richard and Fleetwood had eleven children. When she was confined in April 1610 she was attended by a Dr Jenion who spent seven days at Gawthorpe. He sent in an account for seven pounds, plus 22s 4d for medicines. The midwife came from Wigan and was paid 30s. Her travelling expenses were not entered in the accounts until June so she must have spent several weeks at Gawthorpe. They appear as 'spente by Wllm Woode and Cooke wiffe and towe horses, when they went for the wife of Wigan being a day and a night away, 30s 0d'; and 'spente by Richard Stones when he brought the Wigan wiffe home, and a night away, 21d'. In accordance with an old Lancashire custom Lady Shuttleworth made gifts to other ladies when they were confined. To James Pollard's wife she sent 6s 8d; to a Mrs Sherburne 11s in gold; and to a Mrs Starkie she lent 11s 'when she lay in childbed'.

The ladies of the Shuttleworth family seldom travelled far from home. In August 1610 Lady Shuttleworth, accompanied by her husband, visited their neighbour and relation, Sir Peter Legh; a year later she was in Warwickshire, perhaps Whichford, and two of the bailiffs were sent to escort her home. In August and again in December, 1612, she was at Barton, the home of her girlhood. But the only journey of any consequence she, or any other of the ladies mentioned in the accounts, made was in 1608 when she spent a few months in London. Food for men and horses 'when my Mris and all her companie came to London' amounted to three pounds. To begin with they had lodgings in the Strand, but later a house in Islington was rented at £33 6s 0d a half year, and soon men were being paid to load up the baggage in the Strand and unload it in Islington. James Yate, the steward who was then writing up the accounts, also paid for transporting a box and a bundle of linen from Whichford to London. While in town the ladies seem to have frequently travelled by water. On one occasion they paid 2s for 'a paire of oars'; on another they spent 4d on the return fare to Lambeth; while the waterman who took them to Battersea charged 5s.

At home the ladies did not lack for entertainment. Companies of players acting under the protection of the nobility were still travelling round the country, and the accounts record visits from Lord Morley's players, Lord Essex's players, Lord Dudley's players, and Lord Derby's players. Besides these travelling companies, actors came from Blackburn, Preston, Nantwich, Rochdale, and Cheshire. Usually they were given about 4s. Then there were the itinerant musicians: 'towe pipers' who were given 8d in December 1588; 'the musisiones of Chester' who received 12d in January 1596; and the same sum was given to the piper from Padiham in December 1609 and to 'the Hallifax fiddlers' in March 1610.

On special occasions musicians were summoned to Gawthorpe and were in attendance when, on 18 April 1610, Eleanor Shuttleworth married Ralph Assheton. The bride's dowry was £620 and was paid in six instalments. The marriage must have been a sumptuous one as food bought during April included a Turkey cock, 8 capons, 19 chickens, 7 rabbits, 3 green plover, 2 snipe, a teale, 4 larks, eight score eggs, almonds, butter, sugar, and cakes, as well as 3 gallons and a quart of claret and white wine, and 25 quarts of sack. In addition there were '2 paire of calves feet', presumably to make the jellies that formed an essential part of any festive menu.

On the whole it seems to have been customary for the children's laundry to be sent out to various local women at so much a quarter. In April 1610, Birchall's wife earned 4s for nine months washing for Henry and Lawrence Shuttleworth; in October the cowman's wife received 6d for a quarter's washing for their brother Leigh; in June 1613 two women had 3d 'for starchinge Abell's troueres and Leigh's linnens'; while in the following month 9d was spent on 'washing the cookes boies clothes'. Whether this was the same kitchen boy for whom a doublet and breeches with leather pockets was made in October of the same year, history does not record. A tailor named Smalley was paid 12d for making these garments and 7d for leather and thread.

Servants' wages were paid quarterly and they received in addition an allowance for clothes. Of the female staff the children's nurses seem to have come off best, earning as much as four pounds a year. Compared with the 6s Ellen Seller received for one quarter's service in the kitchen and Jane Clayton the dairymaid's 19s 6d for nine months work, their lot was a happy one, and as each child had its own nurse their duties (presumably they are all wet nurses) cannot have been too exacting.

Careful records were also kept of payments for the family's clothes. In June 1547, 3 doublets, 3 jerkins, and 3 pairs of breeches were made for the boys, and 3 gowns and 3 petticoats for the girls, for an outlay of 4s 8d. Probably Lady Shuttleworth's dresses, like Sir Richard's clothes, came from London. In May 1617 she ordered a cap costing 15s and in July 1621 paid 7s for 'a paire of bodies', that is, for her corset.

The embroiderer who can go from shop to shop in search of materials often wonders how her predecessors managed to clothe themselves and their families, replace their worn out curtains, and renew their household linen. The Shuttleworths bought a variety of materials—cambric, taffeta, fustian, holland, sarcenet, velvet, kersey, saye, russet, and buckram—but do not seem to have gone in for bulk buying and payments are usually for comparatively short lengths purchased for a particular purpose. In 1589, for example, Thomas paid 21s 8d for 13 yards linen 'to be shirts for my brother', and in November 1618 James Burkett was paid 15s for 15 yards of 'tufted stuff' for coats for the children.

The Shuttleworths were an accomplished and well read family. In 1621 they purchased a lute in a case for 25s, a bandore in a case for 35s, 'a little vial' for 4s 7d, and 'a singinge booke' for 2d. They also bought books, school books for the boys, and a copy of Rembert Dodeon's herbal on which John Gerard leaned so heavily when compiling his now more famous herbal. It cost 6s.

Occasionally Lady Shuttleworth bought a few skeins of embroidery silk and also black silk. It was an expensive thread and in 1619 two ounces cost her 4s 8d. From time to time she also purchased 'Coventrie blue thrid' which was used 'to make letters in needlework on the bed-sheets'. It is even more interesting to find that in April 1619 the steward gave 2s 4d to Mr Bradell 'for drowing a waste coate and a night cappe' for her. Possibly this was the waistcoat made up by Pullan and his man in October 1620 for which he charged 2s. Mr Bradell was not, as one might suppose, a pattern drawer, a school master, or some other local person with a talent for drawing. On the contrary he was a man of considerable substance who acted as Receiver General for the King for the Duchy of Lancaster. The Shuttleworths paid him rent for land they leased from the Crown, and when Gawthorpe was being built some of the trees were bought from him. It is difficult, therefore, to see why he should have accepted a fee for drawing an embroidery pattern for his neighbour's wife. The most likely solution seems to be that he had, for some reason, purchased the material for the waistcoat and cap and the money was now being refunded.

During the nineteenth century Gawthorpe was altered by Sir Charles Barry, architect of the Houses of Parliament at Westminster, but in essence it remains virtually unchanged. A few years ago the family handed it over to the care of the National Trust, the Lancashire County Council, and the Nelson and Colne College of Education. Between them they care for the fabric and the grounds, and organise embroidery classes, for it houses a remarkable collection of embroidery and lace made by the Hon Rachel Kay-Shuttleworth who died in 1967. Like William Morris she believed that 'so strong is the bond between history and decoration, that in the practice of the latter we cannot, if we would, wholly shake off the influence of times past over what we do at present.' The collection includes a set of bed furnishings she herself designed and embroidered in crewel wools. Both the design and the stitches are traditional, but nobody could possibly mistake it for traditional crewel work. She has not attempted to be modern, but she has known how to use the past to provide for the present.

Country contentments

As typical of their period as the Shuttleworths of Gawthorpe were the Evelyns of Saye Court at Deptford in Kent, and later of Wotton in Surrey. John Evelyn was a remarkable man, deeply religious, a lover of trees and gardens, a Fellow of Charles II's newly founded Royal Society, and a patron of the arts. Throughout his life he kept a diary for which he is justly famous. His wife, to whom he was devoted, described herself as having 'the care of cakes and stilling and sweetmeats and such useful things', and claimed to have no other desire in the world 'than to perform her duty and promote the welfare of her relations and acquaintances'. Fortunately she was a great letter writer and in one of them we catch an all too rare glimpse—in a woman's own words—of the pattern of her daily domestic life and the multifarious occupations and responsibilities with which it was filled.

> We are willing to acknowledge all time borrowed from family duties is mis-spent; the care of Children's education, observing a Husband's com'ands, assisting the Sick, relieving the Poore, and being serviceable to our Friends, are of sufficient weight to employ the most improved capacities amongst us . . . The Distaff will defend our quarrells as well as the Sword, and the Needle is as instructive as the Penne.

Lest we should be tempted to underestimate Mrs Evelyn's ideas on what 'the most improved capacities of a Lady' might be, it is worth noting that she spoke excellent French and understood Italian, and that her own education can hardly have been less comprehensive than that of her daughter Susannah, of whom her father wrote on her wedding day

> She is a good child, religious, discreet, ingenious, and qualified in all the ornaments of her sex. She has a peculiar talent in designe, as painting in oile and miniature, and an extraordinary talent for whatever hands can do with the needle. She has the French tongue, has read most of the Greek and Roman Authors and Poets, using her talents with great modesty; exquisitely shap'd, and of an agreeable countenance.

In contrast to these quiet, talented ladies there were, of course, any number of frivolous, pleasure seeking people—The Lady New Fashions as one of their sharpest critics, a writer named Barnaby Rich, called them—with painted faces, powdered periwigs, and bold manners. Rich roundly condemns not only the ladies themselves but also the tailors, perfumers, corsetmakers, mercers, and embroiderers who pandered to their vanity and supplied them with expensive laces, silks, satins, and fabrics of gold and silver. He is particularly hard on the merchants who took long and risky journeys in order to fetch home from abroad the 'toies and trifles' they so greatly coveted.

11 Title page of the tenth edition of The Needle's Excellency *printed by James Boler in 1636 and sold by him at the Sign of the Marigold in St Paul's Churchyard.*

Both types are beautifully illustrated in the title page of James Boler's popular pattern book *The Needle's Excellency*. Here, in the middle, is Industry, the lady who sits peacefully in her garden, happily engaged in fashioning some useful garment with her needle. On the left is Wisdom, a tall, thoughtful and withdrawn figure, her mind preoccupied with thoughts inspired by the book she holds between her hands. And on the right is Folly, a distraught, agitated creature with empty, fluttering hands, her unguarded tongue pouring out the latest piece of gossip to her astonished hearers. It is fairly obvious that Folly will embroider only frivolous trifles, many of which she will begin, weary of, and toss on one side. Industry, on the other hand, will make full use of the patterns in Boler's book and be interested in the new fashion for crewel work.

Together with the embroidery pattern books which were first published in Italy during the 1520s, came also little books on household management. One of the most popular was Gervase Markham's *Countrey Contentments* or *The English Hus-wife*, which was first published in 1615 and was still reprinting in 1664. His views on the duties of the good housewife coincide with those of Mrs Evelyn.

> Our English Hus-wife must be of chaste thought, stout courage, patient, untyred, watchful, diligent, witty, pleasant, constant in friendship, full of good neighbourhood, wise in discourse but not frequent therein; sharpe and quick of speech, but not bitter or talkative, secret in her affairs, comfortable in her counsels, and generally skilful in the worthy knowledges that belong to her vocation.

She should, he believed, feed her family on clean, wholesome food 'apter to kill hunger than to revive appetites', and to see that it was set before them regularly. She should know how to clothe them 'outwardly for defence against cold and comeliness of the person, and inwardly for cleanlinesse of the skinne, whereby it may be kept from the filth of sweat or vermin'. In her own dress she was to follow the quiet fashions adopted by modest matrons and avoid 'toyish garnishes and the gloss of light colours'.

It is particularly interesting to discover from Markham's book that the seventeenth century embroiderer had a first-hand knowledge of the spinning and dyeing of her crewel wools, and of the preparation and spinning of linen thread for the warp of the textile on which she used them, that we today may well envy.

With characteristic thoroughness Markham believed that the housewife should know about the fleece from the moment it leaves the sheep's back. He explains how it is to be spread out on a convenient table, and the coarser parts cut off and put on one side to be used later for stuffing quilts; how a certain amount should be reserved to be spun and woven undyed; and how the remainder is to be weighed, put into bags made of netting, labelled, and sent away to be dyed. But although he includes a number of recipes for vegetable dyes, it is clear that he does not expect them to be much used in the home. The Shuttleworths sent their wool to one or other of the dyers in Burnley or Manchester, and in 1619 paid 3s to have 6 yards of cloth dyed orange, while in the following year the dyer at Burnley received 3s 10d for dyeing 11½ yards of cloth 'for the gentlemen's waistcoats'. They also purchased distaff spindles for 4d, a

12 Corner of an eighteenth century bed hanging with unusual design of paired grape vines each growing from a small hillock. For another drawing, see endpaper.

reminder that the spinning wheel was only gradually coming into general use, and that the crewels used for the Bayeux Tapestry and much of the early crewel work were spun on the spindle and distaff. The day of the mechanical Spinning Jenny was still far in the future.

Markham is extremely precise in describing the two different ways in which wool for making cloth was to be spun. For the warp it was to be 'close, round and hard-twisted, strong and well smoothed'; but for the weft which had to blend in together, and did not, as he put it, have to endure the fretting of the heddles, it was to be spun 'open, loose, hollow and but half-twisted'. From this it would seem that the coarser wool that was a feature of much of the crewel work done about 1680 was the same as that used for making the warp of cloth.

overleaf
13 Detail of fence surrounding the tree on the hanging in illustration 22.

overleaf
14 One of the motifs from a picture worked by a little girl named Anna Maria Shirley in 1829. See 'Dutiful daughters'.

15 Part of a bed hanging at Hardwick Hall discussed in Jacobean Embroidery *by Ada Wentworth Fitzwilliam and A.F. Morris Hands (1912).*

16 A crewel work hanging of unusual elegance.

He also believed that the housewife should know about the cultivation and preparation of linen flax. This was not widely grown in England until after 1532, when a law was enacted ordering every landowner of sixty or more acres to put down one rood (about a quarter acre) in flax or hemp. The flax was harvested in late summer, tied in bundles, and set up in a nearby field to dry. Stakes were then driven into the bed of a stream and the bundles laid between them, the pile being covered with planks and stones to prevent them from moving about. In order to remove the seeds from the flax it was beaten or *swingled* on a *swingle tree block* with a *swingle tree dagger*. After a succession of washings, dryings, and beatings, the long fibres came away from the woody stalks and were disentangled and straightened by combing them with a *heckle*. The Shuttleworths grew their flax at Hoole where the soil was light and sandy, and there are frequent payments to both men and women for pulling, swingling, and heckling as well as for spinning and weaving. In September 1584 the wife of Richard Redding who lived at Hoole earned 2s for spinning flax, and in 1617 another woman was paid 20s for weaving 30 yards of 'fyne linnen clothe'. It was linen rather than wool, a smelly, oily material to handle, that the mistress of the house and her daughters usually spun.

But the housewife also had to know how to sow and plant a garden, and in particular to understand the art of *simpling*, that is, the cultivation of herbs and their use in the preparation of medicines. This is perhaps one reason why John Gerard commended his famous *Historie of Plants* as being of particular interest to gentlewomen, and like the good apothecary he was, included in it any number of herbal remedies. If, he wrote, the housewife presses the juice from the leaves of groundsel, adds it to milk, and gives it to her child, it will help relieve its red gums and 'frets'; if she boils them in water or wine and administers a suitable dose to her husband it will 'heal the pain and ache in the Stomack that proceeds from Choler'. Another important part of her housewifely duties was, as Gerard well knew, to grow and gather pot herbs so that in winter she had something with which to flavour otherwise monotonous food. For traditionally, although the orchard was the man's responsibility, the flowers, vegetables, salads, and herbs came within the housewife's province. As old Thomas Tusser put it in his *Five Hundreth Pointes of Good Husbandrie*

> In March and in April from morning to night,
> In sowing and setting, good housewives delight;
> To have in a garden, or other like plot,
> To trim up their house, and to furnish their pot.

By the end of the sixteenth century the lady of the house was also in the habit of picking flowers from her garden and putting them in her rooms. This seems to have greatly pleased a young Dutchman who visited England towards the end of Queen Elizabeth's reign, for he wrote

> Their chambers and parlours strewed with sweet herbs refreshed me; their nosegays finely intermingled with sundry sorts of fragrant flowers in their bed-chambers and privy rooms . . . cheered me up and delighted my senses.

It is a pretty compliment to the good housewife. All in all, she seems to have had an existence that was far from dull. Such time as she had to spare she devoted to practising her accomplishments, one of which might well have been embroidery.

Dutiful daughters

Although all little girls of good family once learnt to do embroidery, it would be as absurd to suppose they all enjoyed it, had any special aptitude for it, or grew up to take more than a casual interest in it, as to think that they all had an ear for music, and eye for colour, a talent for drawing or, like Susannah Evelyn, a gift for languages. But it takes very little imagination to see that before the invention of the domestic sewing machine and the growth of the ready-made garment trade, it was essential that every woman, regardless of her station, should be able to do fine sewing. So we may guess that before she learnt to count out a pattern in prettily coloured silks on her sampler, a girl was taught 'to sew her seam'. That by the time they were twelve many girls could spin the linen thread from which their underclothes were made, is clearly shown in the letters that a girl called Anna Green Winslow wrote to her mother. They were edited by Alice Morse Earle and published in 1894.

Anna Winslow was a descendant of the first woman to jump ashore when the Pilgrim Fathers landed on the coast of North America. In 1770 her parents sent her to Boston to attend a sewing school and a writing school, not as we might suppose to learn embroidery, but to become a neat and dexterous needlewoman. She lodged with a Mrs Demming and her husband whom she called Uncle and Aunt. She was a merry, friendly child, but the hard winters tried her sadly and she suffered from boils and whitlows. Docile and conscientious by nature, she found that when a nasty whitlow made it impossible for her to sew, she could still practise writing and spinning. 'Although I can drive the goose quill a bit, I cannot manage the needle,' she wrote, adding bravely, 'so I will lay my hand to the distaff as the virtuous woman did of old.' A few days later she was able to report: 'My cousin Sally reel'd off a 10 knot skane of yarn today', and a further ten knots were as quickly spun and reeled. Presumably it was the linen woven from this yarn of which she wrote

My aunt gives her love to you, and directs me to tell you that she tho't my piece of linnen would have made me a dozen of shifts, but she could cut no more than ten out of it . . . Nine of them are finish'd, wash'd, and iron'd; and the other would have been done long since if my fingers had not been so sore.

Five days later she put on one of the shifts. Her pride and pleasure were enormous, and she told her mother

By the way, I must inform you (pray do not let papa see this) that yesterday I put on No. 1 of my new shifts and indeed it was very comfortable . . . I don't think I ever had one on before now. It seemed strange, too, to have linnen below my waist.

There is nothing to show that Anna resented the hours she spent her daily 'stent' of plain sewing. On the contrary many of her letters reflect a certain feeling of importance at actively participating in the household needlework. Besides life was not all work and no play. There were dancing classes, visits to friends, romantic stories to read, and a few prim parties called 'constitutions' to which no boy was ever invited. Indeed her chief cause for complaint seems to have been that her clothes were old fashioned and provincial. 'Dear Mama,' she wrote, 'you don't know the fashion here, I beg to look like other folk.'

Although they might pontificate upon the duties of the housewife, no man attempted to describe the techniques of fine sewing and embroidery. But in 1688 a genealogist named Randle Holme included a few brief notes on the schoolmistress and her tools, materials, and teaching methods, in his monumental work *The Academy of Armory and Blazon*. First and foremost she taught

Basting. A slight turning of the Needle and thrid through two pieces of Cloth to keep them together while they are sowed with one of the following stitches: Back Stitch. Fore Stitch. Whip Stitch. Privy Stitch.
Fine Drawing: Sowing two pieces of cloth so curiously together that it cannot be seen where the sowing is.
Ravelling or Roveing: The loosing out of thrids or Silk thrids from a piece of Cloth or Silk.

17 Some embroidery tools illustrated by Randle Holme in The Academy of Armory.

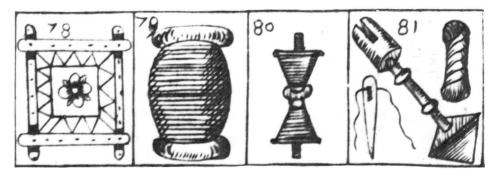

In other words her pupils learnt tacking, seaming, patching and invisible mending. She was also an expert embroiderer and taught sampler making, raised work, gold work and cut work, as well as showing them how to work tent stitch in three different ways: on satin, 'on the finger', and 'on the tent', that is with the linen or canvas stretched on a frame. Besides this she taught net work, by which presumably Holme meant *lacis*, and a number of other methods to which he refers with splendid nonchalance as 'several sorts and manners of works wrought by the Needle with Silk of all Natures, Purle, Wyres, etc. which cannot be described.' He does, however, specifically mention that she used 'Cruel of different Colours' and we may suppose that this was for both canvas work and crewel work.

Once mastered, the techniques of fine sewing are not easily forgotten. On the other hand it is almost impossible for anyone to remember the simplest of re-peating patterns. So, with no other way of recording them, the embroiderer worked them on her sampler, which became her pattern book; and no doubt the child knew from the beginning that in working her sampler she was also forming her own collection of patterns. That she probably made several samplers is clearly shown by a story written by Barnaby Rich, one of the most popular of Elizabethan story tellers. The tale is called *Phylotus and Emilia*.

Phylotus, an aged citizen of Rome, falls in love with the young and beautiful daughter of his friend Alberto, who promises she shall marry him. Knowing protest to be unavailing, Emilia retires to her room and tries to console herself with the advantages she will have as the wife of a wealthy and respected man.

> She remembered how commodious it were to marry one so wealthie as Phylotus whereby she should not need to beate her brains about the practising of housewiferie, but should have servants at commandment to supply that turne; and this pleased her verie well . . . Then she began to think what a pleasure it was to be well furnished with sondrie sutes of apparell, that in the morning, when she should arise, she might call for what she should liste accordyng to the tyme and fasshion did require, and her fancie served her beste: and this likewise pleased her verie well . . . Then each day when she had dined she might go seke out her samplers, *to peruse* whiche would doe beste in a ruffe, whiche in a gorget, whiche on a sleeve, whiche in a quaife, whiche on a caule, whiche in a handkerchief; what lace would do best to edge it, what cutte, what garde: and to sit her down and take it forth little by little, and thus with her needle to pass the afternoone, with devisyng of things for her own wearynge; and this likewise pleased her verie well.

The significant word is, of course, *peruse*. She would read her samplers, turning them over like the pages of a book until she found one that 'pleased her verie well'. She would then 'take it forth little by little', that is, copy it stitch by stitch onto whatever article of dress she needed.

In the sampler is implicit also the ideal of the Good Example: the virtuous lady who is a wise and thrifty housewife as well as a model of perfect behaviour, faithfulness, wisdom, and industry—an example for her daughters to follow as carefully as they copy patterns onto their samplers. One wrongly counted thread spoils the pattern and produces disorder and confusion where all should be coherence and peace. To allow the mind to wander for an instant is to court disaster. To deviate from the model leads only to trouble and unhappiness. The only possible solution is to unpick all the stitches and begin again. William Barley summed it all up in the poem he printed at the beginning of the pattern book he published in 1591

> Then prettie maidens view this prettie book,
> Mark well the works that you therein doe finde:
> Sitting at worke cast not aside your looke,
> They profit small that have a gazing mind:
> Keep cleane your samplers, sleepe not as you sit,
> For sluggishness doth spoile the rarest wit.

The proper place for the sampler is in the embroiderer's work bag where it is readily available for consultation and perusal. It is a fact, however, that both her taste in patterns and her interest or lack of interest in embroidery are reflected on it. The girl who worked the long narrow samplers of the seventeenth century that were rich in both patterns and stitches, grew up to embroider strong patterns, full of invention, in crewel wools; but by the eighteenth century her sampler had changed not only in shape but also in content. Gone were the disciplined, regular repeating patterns and the vigorous stitchery. In their place had come something more nearly resembling a picture or the title page of a prettily illustrated book, with a flowery border round the edge and inside it a scatteration of perky motifs in tent or cross stitch, biblical texts, and pious poetry. The big, curling leaves and stout stems of crewel work had changed too. They had become romantic little posies tied with trailing ribbon bows, touched up with the prevailing taste for the rococo and the fashion for fantastic chinoiserie ornament. They were embroidered in endless concentric lines of tidy, tedious chain stitches or in long and short stitch.

By the nineteenth century, when Berlin work had become synonymous with embroidery and embroiderers had forgotten every interesting stitch in their vocabularies, the sampler had degenerated largely into a dismal collection of alphabets and numerals; no doubt very useful to anyone who, like Lady Shuttleworth, marked her household linen, but useless as a pattern book. Crewel work, as such, had virtually disappeared, and the illustrations in a textbook for teachers called *A Manual of Collective Lessons in Needlework* by Helen K. Brietzcke and Emily F. Rooper show how dreary sewing lessons had become.

First, there is the Needle Drill. The children we are told are too young to distinguish the left from the right hand, so a piece of red cotton is tied round one and a piece of black round the other. Enter John Right and Susan Left. On the command 'One!' Susan Left picks up the needle, touches her mouth with it, and holds it straight out six inches in front of her. On the word 'Two!' John Right takes the thread and puts it through the eye of the needle while the teacher counts to thirty. Desperately he hopes it will go cleanly through. If it does not he will soon be found out, for on the word 'Three!' he must take the needle and slide it to the middle of the thread. On 'Four!' he and Susan each pick up an

The Needle Drill.

At the word "four" each *end* of the cotton is held, and the needle is seen dangling on the cotton.

The Marking Lesson.

20 Learning to work the Marking Stitch.

end of the thread and hold it high up in the air so that the needle can be seen to dangle freely from it. Then the unbelievable happens. At the word 'Five!' the thread is pulled out of the needle, and at 'Six!' both needle and thread are laid side by side on the desk. At 'Attention!' both hands are clasped behind the back.

Next there is the Marking Stitch. The stitches march and countermarch across a demonstration frame made by the teacher as a helpful parade ground. Have you counted the correct number of threads? Is the wrong side as neat as the right? Then out it all comes and we begin again. It is all rather discouraging for the inexpert. Some of the samplers get grubby and crumpled; others stay irritatingly pristine. Why should some have tiny blood stains and others not? Why must there be no whispering, no friendly nudging of the neighbour on the uncomfortable backless bench? Retribution is swift and embarrassing. There they are, poor little things, conspicuous and convicted; prisoners in their corner, their aprons draped over their heads like some mournful widow's weeds.

Looking at the pictures it is hard to believe that before the end of the century crewel work will have come into its own again, and that new and more liberal methods of embroidery teaching will have been planned, out of which will grow the desire of innumerable embroiderers to become the creators of their own designs.

A peculiar talent for design

It is difficult to imagine ladies of households similar to those presided over by Lady Shuttleworth or Mrs Evelyn setting out to compose the patterns for a set of bed hangings which, if those worked by Abigail Pett can be taken as typical, consisted of two curtains 6 feet 3 inches long and 7 feet 3 inches wide (that is, 5 widths of $18\frac{1}{2}$ inch material); two other curtains of the same length, measuring 3 feet 3 inches wide (that is, $2\frac{1}{2}$ widths of $17\frac{1}{2}$ inch material); and four valances, all $8\frac{1}{2}$ inches deep, two of which were 6 feet 1 inch long, and the other two 4 feet 7 inches long. All other considerations apart, the problem of transferring the design (which might daunt the most ambitious embroiderer today, even allowing for her modern drawing aids and rolls of drawing and tracing paper) seems almost certainly to have been well beyond their capacity or desire.

Of course, if her bent lay in that direction, the seventeenth or eighteenth century embroiderer might invent a pattern for a work bag, a stomacher, a cushion cover, or a pair of pockets, and undoubtedly some, like Mrs Mary Delany, did. She was, however, far more likely to copy a small pattern from another embroidery, or compose one from 'slips' or detached motifs, a taste for which she inherited from her Elizabethan forbears. But on balance we must decide that much of her larger pieces of crewel work were prepared for her by the successors of the artists who drew the design for the Bayeux Tapestry and who, as 'pattern drawers' feature in the household accounts of establishments such as those maintained by the Countess of Shrewsbury at Chatsworth and subsequently at Hardwick.

The business of pattern drawing was not unprofitable. It was described in 1747 in a book entitled *The London Tradesman* prepared by a man named R. Campbell as a guide for young men and women who were seeking employment with one or other of the craftsmen with workrooms or studios in the city. But drawing patterns 'to please the Changeable Foible of the Ladies' was only a minor part of the pattern drawer's work which, Campbell disparagingly remarks, could be entrusted to any boy with the slightest disposition towards drawing; the more talented and experienced employees being engaged in drawing patterns for professional embroiderers as well as for lacemakers, quilters, and textile printers. He noted that, unlike many other craftsmen, business was pretty constant throughout the year and was at its height during the season when 'the Company are in Town', and that, once out of his apprenticeship, a journeyman could earn as much as 25 to 30 shillings a week. The embroiderer in pursuit of a pattern, could, if she wished, visit him in his studio (which is probably what most workroom managers did), but the majority of ladies dealt with him through the agency of their favourite haberdasher.

Originally a vendor of a miscellaneous collection of small goods, the haberdasher had, by the sixteenth century, emerged as a retailer of costume accessories, laces, ribbons, and so on. His business was intricate and detailed and his principal customer was the tailor whom he supplied with buckram, tape, fastenings, thread, and other essentials of his trade. The embroiderer went to him for her needles, pins, thimbles, silks, gold wires, and crewels. Although his wares were small in scale he was not necessarily in a small way of business. On the contrary, the five medieval burgesses who appear briefly in the Prologue to *The Canterbury Tales*—the Haberdasher, the Weaver, the Tapestry Weaver, the Dyer, and the Carpenter—were all men of considerable substance whom Chaucer thought well qualified to become aldermen and masters of their respective guilds. He slyly observed that their wives would no doubt enjoy being called 'Madame' and having their trains carried on festive occasions as though they were princesses.

By the seventeenth century it was customary for shopkeepers to display painted signs above their doors, and before long they were issuing handbills or trade cards on which they advertised their address, the type of goods they kept in stock, and the nature of the services they were prepared to offer to their customers. The device on these cards was often a replica of the sign above their door.

For the embroiderer, a haberdasher named Elizabeth Barton Stent kept a line of ivory thimbles, needle cases, and pounce boxes, and many others announced their willingness to draw patterns for her. Abraham Pinhorn, for example, who married Lydia Tidmarsh in Lincoln's Inn Chapel on 16 December 1731, drew 'all sorts of Patterns for Needlework, French Quilting, Embroidery, Cross and Tent Stitch', and sold 'shades of Silk and Worsted' for working them; while a year later Marmaduke Smith proudly announced the opening of 'an entirely new Collection of Patterns for Ladies' Work', including some for canvas work chair seats, screens, and carpets. On 7 June he sent out an account on the back of one of his trade cards which gives an idea of the contemporary charges for pattern drawing.

2 yards wide canvas	4s od
Drawing 2 Seats for Chairs	5s od
Canvas and Drawing for 2 Seats for small Chairs	5s od

But not all ladies lived in London within easy access of a good pattern drawer, or even came up for the Season; and for the embroiderer who, like Lady Shuttleworth, seldom travelled far from her husband's country estate, the problem of getting her patterns drawn was a very real one. A handful of letters written by Lady Brilliana Harley from her home at Brampton Bryan Castle near Ludlow, on the Herefordshire border, show how quick she was to take advantage of every opportunity to get her patterns drawn and replenish her store of embroidery threads. They were published by the Campden Society in 1853.

Lady Brilliana was twenty three when, on 22 July 1623, she became the third wife of Sir Robert Harley, a staunch upholder of the Puritan cause, who served in the Roundhead army, and was subsequently appointed by Parliament to act as official receiver of the monies raised from the sale of the gold and jewels recovered from the fires into which the iconoclasts were to throw the medieval vestments with which English Cathedrals were so richly endowed. It seems a curious office for the wife of so enthusiastic an embroiderer to hold.

Brilliana Harley was a well educated woman who knew Latin and preferred to read in French rather than English. As parliamentary duties kept her husband away from home for long periods of time, she had to manage not only the household but also the estate, and her letters to him are full of a nice mixture of tender solicitude for his welfare and news about the day to day happenings on the farms. She wrote about the sowing and reaping of crops, the livestock, the unseasonable weather, and the tenants whom she ruled with kindly despotism. That the times were evil troubled her conscience greatly, but a supreme trust in the over-ruling providence of God comforted and sustained her, even when in 1644 the castle was beseiged for many weeks by the Royalist forces, and she was compelled to defend it against them.

When her son Edward took up residence at Oxford, he was accompanied by a young man named George Griffiths who, in exchange for acting as his servitor, could attend lectures at the university. They were a remarkable pair. George was to become one of the leaders of the non-conformist movement in England, while Edward's son, Robert Harley, who was created first Earl of Oxford, was destined to be Queen Anne's most trusted minister. Meantime, one of George's duties was to execute commissions for Lady Harley.

On 22 March 1638, she wrote to Edward asking him to tell George Griffiths that she had sent him the money owing to 'Mr Neelham the drawer' and bidding him remind the man that she 'would have him hasten the sending of the piece of cloth he had to draw'. Either Mr Nelham (or Neelham) was dilatory or else he undertook more work than he could cope with for, on 14 March 1639, she wrote again to Edward asking him to tell George that although she had received 'the petticoate that Mr Nelham did drawe, and the silke and wyre', she was not prepared to pay for them until she received a piece of green cloth for which she had clearly grown tired of waiting.

Like other sons, Edward seems to have taken an interest in his mother's embroidery for on 25 June 1641, she wrote to thank him for a pattern he had sent her from London.

> I thank you for the patterne of worke you sent me. I like it very well and if it please God I propose to woorke a shute of chars [a set of chairs] of it, and I hope you will enjoy them.

As always, she signed herself

Your most affectionate Mother,
Brilliana Harley

21 Lady Brilliana Harley's signature

Poor lady, her health had been sadly undermined by the privations she had endured during the seige of the castle and on 9 October 1643, she wrote to Edward for the last time telling him

> I have taken a very greate coold, which has made me very ill for 2 or 3 days, but I hope the Lord will be merciful to me, in giving me my health, for it is an ill time to be sick in.

But her prayers were not granted, and a few days later she died.

Plainly George Griffiths was not dealing with Mr Nelham through a haberdasher, but directly with the man himself. Indeed there seems to have been no haberdasher in Oxford of this name at the time. This being so, it is unexpected to find that he could supply Lady Harley with embroidery silks and gold thread. Probably he had discovered that it served both his own and his clients' best interests if he himself carried a supply of threads for working the patterns he drew for them. This being so, it is likely that if the embroiderer could not get into Oxford to select her own colours, he may well have made the choice himself. To all intents and purposes he was, therefore, providing a seventeenth century version of the modern embroidery kit.

In August 1770 when *The Ladies' Magazine*, after several abortive attempts, began its long life, the embroiderer stumbled upon a new and apparently inexhaustable supply of patterns. In her preface to the first issue the editor announced that it was her intention to publish needlework patterns for her readers.

Our Patronesses will find in the Magazine, Price only Six-Pence, among other variety of Copper-Plates [illustrations], a Pattern that would cost them double at the Haberdashers': and by the progressive improvement in pattern-drawing to furnish them with drawings that will show the elegance of their Taste, and their own perfection in handling the Needle.

The patterns were printed on long, pull-out pages and the fact that so few survive bears witness to their popularity. But the editor was not really interested in embroidery. Indeed the time was not far off when she would use the needle as the badge of the domestic servitude she was to exhort her readers to rebel against. Meanwhile, with sound business acumen, she recognised in the embroidery pattern a useful device for increasing the sale of her magazine, trapping her readers into thinking they were getting that irresistible thing—a free gift. It is interesting that so successful was the idea that when some sixty years later Godey introduced his *Lady's Book* to the American public, he should have used exactly the same sales promotion gimmick. The resourceful Samuel Beeton played a similar trick in his *Englishwoman's Domestic Magazine*.

But everybody was happy. The subscribers felt they had not only a good bargain but also a regular monthly supply of patterns; and the pattern drawer was no doubt delighted to find himself with so flourishing a new outlet for his designs. Nevertheless, the seeds sown so casually in the summer of 1770 bore some strangely disturbing fruit. From them sprang the mass produced embroidery leaflets and magazines later to be put out by the manufacturers of embroidery threads and materials to advertise their wares. With them came a new line in crewel work patterns, many so debilitated by constant re-drawing that it is often difficult to recognise the seventeenth century design from which they were originally copied. Their 'quaintness' outraged the twentieth century embroiderer, strengthening her determination to make herself independent of the pattern drawer by learning to compose her own designs.

overleaf
22 Tall palm tree surrounded by an irregular fence and supported on either side by wavy branches bearing exotic flowers and leaves. A Chinese phoenix perches on the left hand branch. Detail from illustration 13.

Entr'acte II

And as this booke some cunning workes doth teach,
(Too hard for meane capacities to reach)
So for weake learners, other workes here be,
As plaine and easie as are A B C.
Thus skilful, or unskilled, each may take
This booke, and of it each good use may make,
All sortes of workes, almost that can be nam'd,
Here are directions how they may be fram'd:
And for this kingdomes good are hither come,
From the remotest partes of Christendome,
Collected with much paines and industrie,
From scorching *Spaine* and freezing *Muscovie*,
From fertill *France*, and pleasant *Italy*,
From *Poland, Sweden, Denmark, Germany*,
And some of these rare patternes have been fetch'd
Beyond the bounds of faithlesse *Mohamet*:
From spacious *China* and those kingdomes East,
And from great *Mexico*, the Indies West.
Thus are these workes, *farrefetcht* and *dearly bought*,
And consequently *good for ladies thought*.

John Taylor, In Praise of the Needle

After the Bayeux Tapestry there are no more surviving examples of English crewel work for six hundred years. In this very long period of time the world as we know it began. Westminster Abbey, where Edward the Confessor was buried and where William the Conqueror was crowned, was completed. The embroiderers in the royal workrooms furnished it with hangings and banners of samite, and vestments that shimmered with gold and jewels. They made the Syon cope, the Clare chasuble, and the John of Thanet panel.

Magna Carta was signed and the day of the feudal barons came to an end. With them went strongly fortified castles and keeps like Pevensey and Dover. Moats dried up and drawbridges disappeared. By turning the castle walls inside out and pushing the rooms together into a single block, men built spacious, comfortable manor houses. Their windows no longer faced inwards onto a central courtyard, but with bold assurance their owners looked out through them over the surrounding countryside. Battlements from which men had once poured down a hail of stones and arrows upon their attackers were no longer needed for protection, so they became decorative and turned into parapets around the housetops behind which sprouted a thicket of highly ornamental chimneys. The secluded garden within the castle walls ceased to exist. In its place came arbours and pleached alleys, clipped yews, and little geometric borders outlined in low growing, sweet smelling hedges, that people called knots. The embroiderer and the lacemaker repeated these entwined patterns on their own work.

After the Renaissance men looked at the world differently. They had finished with medievalism. The day of the merchant princes had arrived, and from the orient merchandise poured into the Levantine markets and from them to Venice, which rose to a position of unrivalled commercial eminence. Her doges and procurators built palaces for themselves along the Grand Canal; their warehouses overflowed with silks and spices; they clothed themselves in robes of fur and velvet and became patrons of the arts. Once a year they celebrated symbolically the marriage of their proud and beautiful city with the sea whence came their power and wealth.

Infuriated by Venice's monopoly of the Far Eastern trade and bled white by the taxes she imposed upon the other nations who came to buy from her, Spain and Portugal began to search for the fabled sea route to India and China. Convinced that if he sailed far enough west he must land on the coast of China, Christopher Columbus discovered the new world of America, and in 1488, Bartholomew Diaz de Noaves edged his way cautiously around the Cape of Good Hope, and pressed on far enough up the coast to satisfy himself that he had indeed found the way to India. He was quickly followed by Vasco da Gama who, with four little ships, sailed up the east coast of Africa as far as Malindi where the trade route from India terminated. Here he picked up the necessary local information about tides, winds, and currents from other captains, and in May 1498 landed at Calicut on the west coast of India. A new word entered the English vocabulary—*calico*.

Where Portugal had led, other European countries were bound to follow. In 1505 an English company of Merchant Adventurers was set up to trade with the Far East, but it was not until the last day of December 1600 that the aged Queen Elizabeth signed the charter incorporating the East India Company, an agreement that her successor James I was only too happy to endorse.

In 1612 the Mughul rulers of the State of Gurjarat on the Coromandel coast agreed to the East India Company's setting up of a trading post at Surat. By 1658 it was the largest factory in the area, and in 1687 the Company's headquarters was transferred to Bombay, which Portugal had ceded to England as part of the dowry of Catherine da Braganza when she married Charles II. Completely ignorant of the geography of the Far East, even the Lord Chancellor,

Thomas Cromwell did not realise what a good bargain England had got. When asked in which direction this newly acquired land lay, he replied with splendid assurance: 'It is a paltry island a little distance off the coast of Brazil.' It was just this sense of unreality, mystery, and unknowing that enchanted the west. They loved the luminous silks, the rich embroideries, the jewels and pearls, the aromatic spices and perfumes, and the porcelain and lacquer work that came sailing up the English Channel in the holds of the East India Company's ships. Avidly they collected them in their cabinets of curiosities. With them came the curiously painted cottons called *pintadoes*, *palampores* and *chints* that were to usher in a new phase in the history of crewel work.

The old and the new

In 1561 a Newcastle merchant called John Wilkinson became mayor of the city. The inventory of his possessions made at the time of his death was published by the Surtees Society in 1834. The stock in his Great Shoppe included such interesting items as

> a qr of a lb and a ounce of collor thread
> iii ounces of collor silk
> i ounce and ½ of cole black silk
> i ounce and ½ of cording for poises
> iii c and ½ of thymbles
> xiii clowtes of tailer nedles
> vi clowtes of fyne semster nedles
> iii clowtes of cowrse nedles
> xx papers of great pynnes
> viii yeardes of fyne canwes
> vii yeardes and ½ of cowser canwes
> iii yeardes in remlants of canwes

as well as a good deal of black and russet stitching silk; white, russet, and black sewing silk; sewing silk of all colours, and both coarse and fine gold thread;

while in his Lytle Shop were yards and yards of fine woollen cloth in 'sky collor', black, white, yellow, and 'shep' colour, together with eight pounds of sewing crewel valued at 20 shillings.

Naturally the subject of needles is of great interest to the embroiderer. She has her stalwart tapestry needles with long, accommodating eyes and blunt points, and her crewel needles with smaller, shorter eyes and sharp points. Her predecessors must have needed equally strong needles with good big eyes for the heavy wools characteristic of much of the crewel work made about 1696, according to a date discovered by Mrs Katherine Brett of the Royal Ontario Museum, Toronto, on a piece in the collection [34]. Fortunately in *The Academy of Armory* Randle Holme gave a list of needles being manufactured at this time. They included glovers' needles, bookbinders' needles, surgeons' needles, and what were, presumably, sewing and embroidery needles which he describes as 'ordinary needles'; 'pearl needles' which seem to have been very fine indeed, and needles ranging in size from one to ten. Exactly where Mr Wilkinson's 'cowrse needles' fit into this classification it is, of course, impossible to know, but it seems an apt description to apply to a needle that was going to be threaded with crewel wool like that used on hangings contemporaneous with the Toronto example.

Plainly if it was not Mr Wilkinson himself then it was some other local haberdasher who supplied needles, wool, and canvas to Mrs Elizabeth Hutton, widow of John Hutton of Hinwick Hall, the inventory of whose possessions was also published by the Surtees Society in 1834. In the High Great Chamber of her house were two testers 'with curtens of croole' which must have been much worn for they were valued at only one shilling; a table carpet worth 33 shillings that was five yards long and a yard and a half in width; two small cushions and two long cushions worked in crewels; and an unfinished table carpet 'with crooles for the same' valued at six pounds. Mrs Hutton was, it seems, devoted to canvas work and thought nothing of setting to work on such a large scale project as a table carpet, but whether she or any other lady in similar circumstances would have wished to spoil her hands by using the harsher of the crewel wools is a matter for conjecture. Her skin, if it was at all fine, would certainly have been much roughened, and would have made embroidery with silk thread impossible for a long time. On balance it seems likely, therefore, that some at least of the larger surviving examples of crewel work were made by professional embroiderers who, once again, may have included men.

Quite apart from the fact that embroidery in crewel wools and surface stitchery as distinct from canvas work had not been fashionable for many a long day, and was no doubt due for a revival, it was only to be expected that ladies holding the same ideals as those of Gervase Markham and Mrs Evelyn would sooner or later discover in themselves a taste for plain down-to-earth twill and homely crewel wools, and would adapt their well tried and familiar coiling patterns and their pretty flowers to a larger scale and less refined method. Indeed there is little to choose between the pattern on the black work petticoat in the London Museum [23] and the bed hangings from Cotehele House in Cornwall [29]. To all intents and purposes the embroiderer has taken one of her crewel work hangings, wrapped it round her waist, and called it a petticoat;

23 *Black work skirt in the London Museum. Compare with illustration 29.*

and the process could have been carried out equally well the other way round. What is so striking about these early crewel work patterns is first that they are largely monochromatic, and second that, like so much Elizabethan embroidery, the patterns are more nearly related to textile design than to embroidery. Plainly, the embroiderer has had nothing to say to the idea that the pattern should relate to the shape of the curtain, as the later patterns do, but has simply taken a length of material and covered it from end to end and from selvedge to selvedge with needlework; her only concession being that she has generally contained the pattern within a narrow, ribbon-like border.

The few surviving examples of early crewel work have fascinated both the embroiderer and the scholar. In 1909, inspired partly by a desire to promote the sale of their embroidery threads and patterns and partly to test the market for a high quality periodical on embroidery, James Pearsall & Company financed the publication of a series of articles issued in six parts under the title *Embroidery*. The editor was Mrs A. H. Christie whose first book *Embroidery and Tapestry Weaving* had been published three years previously. In the sixth number she printed an article by William R. Lethaby on the Bayeux Tapestry and another by A. F. Kendrick on a striking example of crewel work that had just been acquired by the Victoria and Albert Museum [32]. Then in 1922 the same firm, this time in conjunction with the Old Bleach Linen Company, sponsored the publication of a magazine called *The Embroideress*. It enjoyed a long life going out of business only on the outbreak of war in 1939. The editor was Mrs M. E. Rolleston, later to be joined by Mrs Kathleen Harris, who subsequently contributed so much to *Embroidery*, the journal of the Embroiderers' Guild, publication of which commenced in 1932.

For the third issue of *The Embroideress*, Mrs Rolleston wrote an article entitled 'A Rare Example of Seventeenth Century Embroidery'. The subject was a curtain measuring 77 by 41 inches and worked throughout in blue-green crewels.

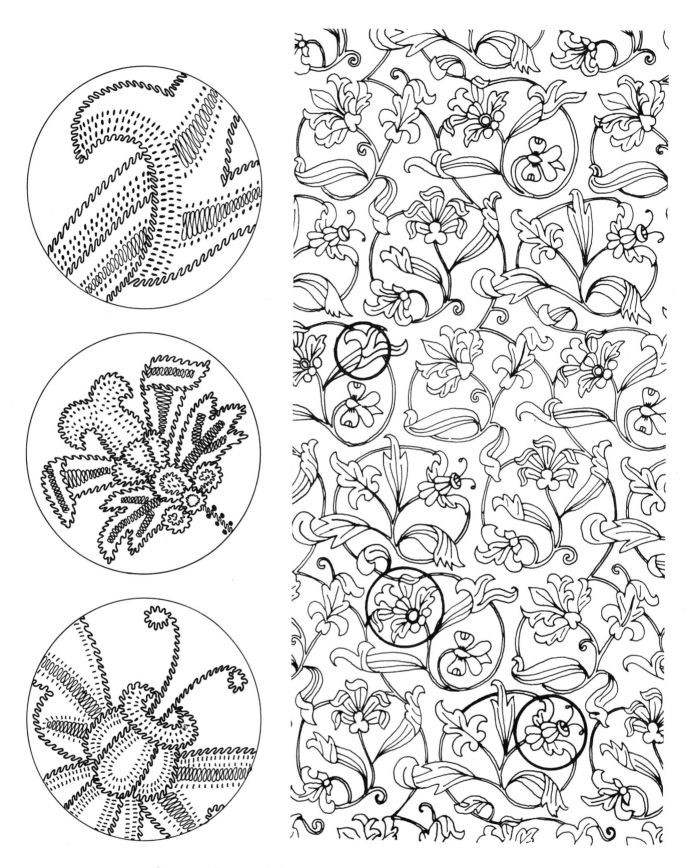

24 A seventeenth century bed curtain with coiling stems enclosing stylised lilies and honey-suckle flowers. Each repeat measures approximately 16 inches square.

25 *Work bag made in 1672 in stem, satin, herringbone, coral, buttonhole, and link stitches.*

It belonged to Mrs Lewis F. Day, wife of the well known designer who, in 1900, had published a book—*Art in Needlework*—in which he encouraged the embroiderer to learn to draw her own patterns, but warned that to insist too strenuously that the designer and the embroiderer should always be one and the same person was to set up an ideal difficult to fulfil. 'You can only make all the world designers', he wrote, 'by reducing design to what all the world can do. And that is not very much.'

The designer of Mrs Day's curtain had been no amateur. The pattern is dignified and at the same time alive with invention and variety [26]; a collection of curling ostrich feathers, set against a background of coiling stems bearing tiny pea-like flowers, and scattered with regularly spaced dots.

Mrs Rolleston was able to report that in 1898 Mrs Conyers Morrell, editor of *Home Art Work*, had published a detail from an identical curtain in the form of a working drawing of one of the feathers, showing the stitches in which it had been embroidered. For some reason she called it the Amy Robsart Plume Pattern.

Obviously Mrs Rolleston's curiosity had been stirred by the unusual design, and it is not difficult to imagine her satisfaction when, in the seventeenth issue of *The Embroideress*, she was able to produce another plumed pattern. This time she found it in a collection of Elizabethan embroidery patterns included by Thomas Trevelyon in his Miscellany or commonplace book, a copy of which had been sold at Sotheby's in 1923. It came into the possession of Mrs Pierpoint Morgan who gave a set of photographs of the patterns to Mrs Guy Antrobus, a collector, embroiderer, and staunch supporter of the Embroiderers' Guild. She in turn passed the photographs on to Mrs Rolleston. The design is stiffer and more formal than Mrs Day's, and the feathers far less decorative [27].

Like everybody else the Elizabethan embroiderer believed that the ostrich could eat iron, and it appears in canvas work on one of the cruciform medallions on the Oxburgh hangings, with a horseshoe in its beak and a scroll on which is written *The Estriche* (see page 80). Using them no doubt as symbolic of mourning and sadness, Mary Queen of Scots placed a semi-circle of ostrich feathers around the armillary globe that she worked in tent stitch on the panel for the centre of one of the other hangings; above is a scroll whose message is best translated as 'Sorrows pass but Hope endures'; while on a matching panel, worked by Bess of Hardwick in memory of her husband Sir William Cavendish, she put an ostrich feather fan from which a few of the feathers have fallen, knowing that everybody would realise she was making clever play with two French words: *penne* meaning plume, and *peine* meaning grief (see page 80).

Finally, in the twentieth issue of *The Embroideress* Mrs Rolleston reproduced a very different type of crewel work pattern with an article by A. F. Kendrick entitled 'A Stuart Bed Curtain' [28]. Each unit consists of a spray of flowers set in a vase of classical or renaissance type, enclosed in a narrow rope or plait from which hangs a pair of flowers. It is repeated all over the curtain like a textile design. Kendrick compares the curtain to a work bag, dated 1672 and worked in rose red crewels [25], and the motifs on this back again to the detached 'slips' beloved by the Elizabethan embroiderer for canvas work. The scholar thus proves to the embroiderer that her crewel work grows naturally out of earlier and well established conventions of English embroidery.

26 Detail of pattern on Mrs Lewis F. Day's curtain as reproduced in The Embroideress.

27 *Plumes and foxgloves from Thomas Trevelyon's Miscellany of 1608, reproduced from the* The Embroideress.

28 Detail of all-over pattern from a seventeenth century bed hanging. Each repeat consists of a classical vase filled with flowers and contained within a continuous linked chain.

29 Bed at Cotehele House, Cornwall. Compare with illustration 23.

The difficulty of distinguishing professional from domestic embroidery is a very real one. Fortunately, some of the work bags embroidered in crewel wools are so frank, casual, and engaging that it would be hard to imagine them as anything but domestic. On one [30] the embroiderer has used detached motifs typical of Elizabethan canvas work and has worked them in a technique associated with black work—that is, with a strong outline shaded with seeding or speckling. Furthermore she has chosen motifs symbolic of the attributes of the virtuous lady. Here she stands in the centre, an open book in one hand on which the word 'Faith' is written, and in the other a lighted candle indicating that she walks through life by the light of faith. In each corner is a detached motif or 'slip', roughly the same size as the figure itself. Then there are other smaller 'slips' filling up the spaces between: the pelican in her piety, the strawberry for righteousness, the pansy for meditation, and part of a carnation for love. Between them again is a crowd of smaller motifs: the snail for laziness, moths for the evanescence of human life, silk worms for industry, and bees for diligence and orderliness. But whether it is intended that we should read the motifs for their hidden meaning, or whether the embroiderer chose them simply because she liked them, is as impossible to say as it is to know for certain whether she found them in a book and arranged them herself, or bought the bag 'traced ready for working' from a haberdasher or pattern drawer.

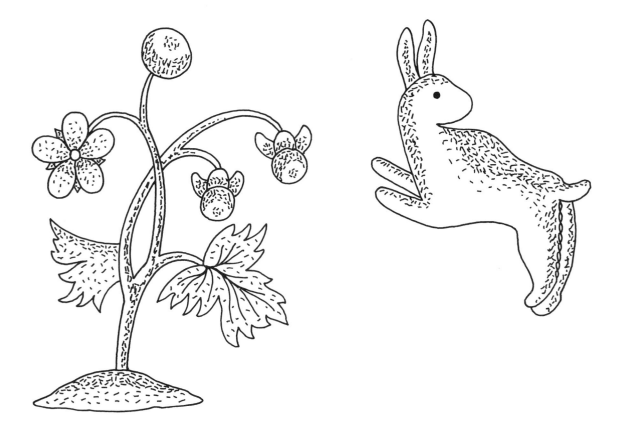

30 Work bag with typical English motifs in stem, back, and link stitches, with speckling. The pattern is repeated on the other side but the lady is dressed differently and carries an anchor.

To devise a pattern like this by pushing a collection of motifs of assorted sizes about like the pieces of a jig-saw puzzle until some balance and order emerges, is well within the capacity of most embroiderers. But for her to try to make a repeating pattern to fill a given space is quite another thing. The effort nearly defeated the far from expert draughtsman who drew the pattern on the other work bag in illustration 31. Possibly it is a not very successful copy of another embroidery pattern. The coiling stems shooting out from their undersized hillocks that long to join smoothly into one another but are unable to decide how to do it, the limp worm-like leaves twisted round them, and the eccentrically placed branches, all betray the inexperienced designer up to the neck in trouble. The day has been saved by the embroiderer's competent stitchery. This delight in stitchery for its own sake that is typical of the English embroiderer, together with a restrained and often monochromatic use of colur, is the hallmark of many of the earlier surviving examples of seventeenth century crewel work.

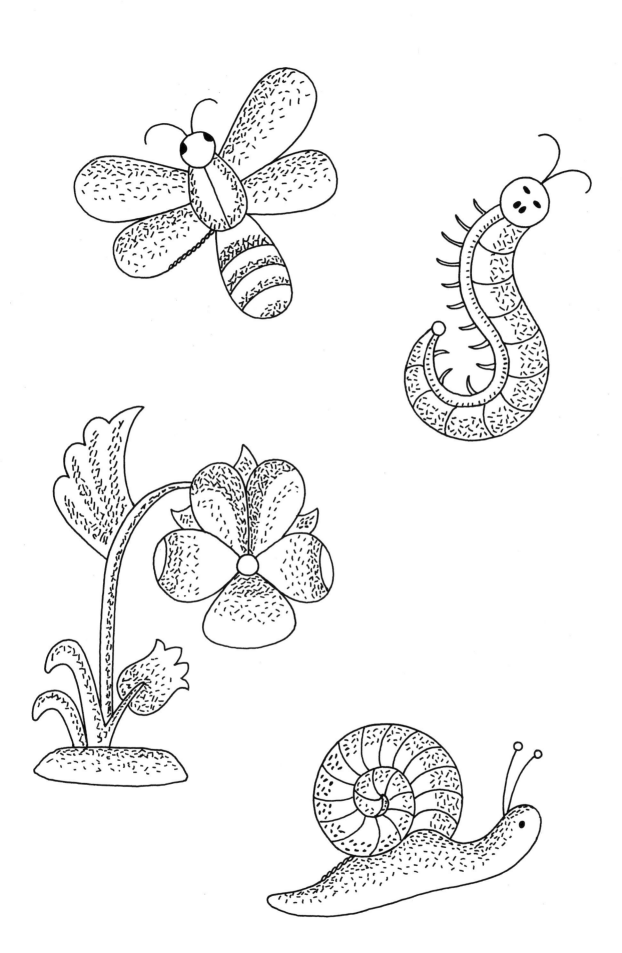

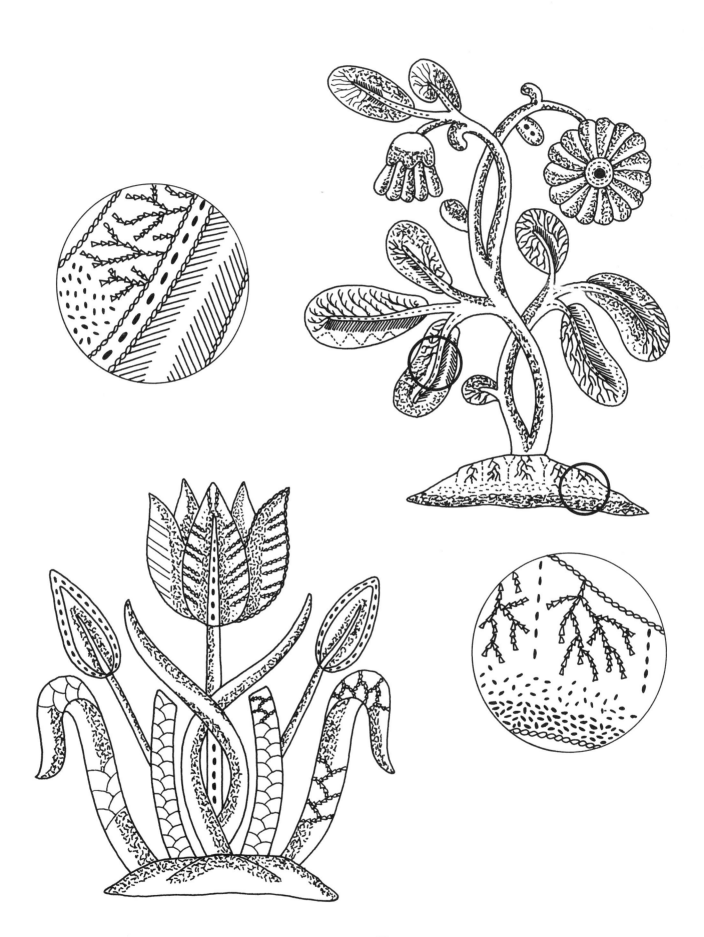

East of the sun
and west of the moon

Among the decorative arts the role of the embroiderer is generally reckoned to be a relatively minor one. She is always there, however, a shadowy figure in the wings, watching the great artists and designers, the originators of new styles and fashions, squaring up to the footlights and taking their curtain calls. Somewhat belatedly she brings her own patterns into line with theirs. Only rarely is she caught by a wandering spotlight in the act of producing such miracles of invention as the medieval vestments or the Elizabethan black work sleeves. Even less often does she embroider a pattern of such importance to scholars as the Bayeux Tapestry, or of such interest to textile historians as the fragment of a crewel work hanging of about 1680 which is now in the Boston Museum of Fine Arts [33], the pattern on which plainly comes from the same source as that on a painted cotton hanging in the Victoria and Albert Museum [35], made at roughly the same date somewhere on the west coast of India.

Hangings painted on cloth saturated with gum and mounted on a coarse woollen textile were a feature of the furnishings of a Tudor house. In the same year that the Surtees Society published the inventories of John Wilkinson and Mrs Hutton, it also published the will of Sir Thomas Hilton of Hilton Castle. Among his possessions was a set of 'hangings of painted cloth'. Probably the patterns on them were much the same as those described by William Harrison who travelled up and down the country during the reign of Queen Elizabeth. He found the houses hung with painted cloths on which were depicted 'divers histories' or else patterns of 'hearbes, beasts, knots and such-like', while in a letter dated 14 August 1585, William Cecil, Elizabeth's Lord Treasurer, described a set at his home at Theobalds in Hertfordshire, which consisted of a double row of six trees having 'the natural bark so artificially joined with birds' nests and leaves as well as fruit upon them, all managed in such a manner that you could not distinguish between the natural and these artificial trees'; claiming that when the windows were opened 'the birds flew into the hall, perched themselves upon the branches and began to sing'. So it is clear that long before the directors of the East India Company began to import painted hangings from India, the English embroiderer was accustomed to furnishing her rooms, not only with tapestries, but also with prettily painted hangings, the patterns on which must often have been similar to those she worked on her embroidery. By comparison the Indian patterns must have seemed crude and unattractive. Besides, they were quite unlike what she expected oriental patterns to look like, being accustomed to those sold by haberdashers, such as George Paravicini, one of whose trade cards was collected by that master hoarder, Samuel Pepys. Paravicini described himself as 'A Pinker, Cutter and Raiser of Sattin' and offered to draw not only patterns for bed hangings, quilts, petticoats, and waistcoats, but also 'all sorts of Indian Patterns' which he probably expected to sell to japanners, textile printers and embroiderers. As Pepys died in 1703, the patterns provided by Paravicini may well have been in the same style as those on the crewel work fragment in Boston and the Ashburnham hanging in the Victoria and Albert Museum.

The patterns on the first palampores to reach England were rendered in white on a coloured ground. The directors of the East India Company found that a few people bought them as curiosities but were disappointed to find that beyond this there was no great sale for them. Accordingly they instructed their factors in Surat to get the Indians to reverse the process, hoping that coloured patterns on a white ground would prove more popular.

> More should be made with white grounds and the branches and flowers to be in collors and not to be (as those last sent) all in general of deep redd ground and other sadder collors.

Still the market remained no more than lukewarm. It could hardly be otherwise. Knowing little or nothing about the geography of the Far East, the English naturally imagined that all oriental art was the same. That the art of China, on which they had for centuries based their fanciful ideas about what the orient was like and which had to a certain extent already begun to influence their own patterns, could possibly be completely different from the art of India never for one instant occurred to them. The directors decided that the only way to promote the sale of their palampores was to send out to the factors in India patterns which, although basically English, were—to borrow an apt but rather later phrase—'in the Chinese taste'. So by 1670 it is not surprising to read that a French visitor to India, Jean Baptiste Tavernier, could observe that the Indians were painting their calicoes from patterns given to them by European merchants.

This time the results exceeded the directors' wildest hopes. In 1665 John Evelyn visited Lady Mordaunt at her home in Ashstead and was interested to find that she had a room hung with pintadoes. He had good reason to be grateful for the prosperity of the East India Company. On 27 November 1657, he had

31 Work bag made during the second half of the seventeenth century in stem, satin, herringbone, coral, buttonhole, link, braid, and long and short stitches, with speckling.

32 Late seventeenth century bed hanging worked in very thick crewel wool. A large leaf disguises the weak spot in the design where the heavy branches cross.

invested £500 in the Company. Now, in 1682, he sold them to the Royal Society, noting with satisfaction in his diary that the investment had been 'extraordinarily advantageous'.

A year later the delighted directors wrote to Surat, 'You cannot imagine what a great number of Chintses would sell here', ordering the factors to send forthwith

> 100 suits of painted curtains and vallances ready made up of several sorts and prices, strong but none too deare, nor any over mean in regard,

for, they added, only the poorest people in England now lay in beds without curtains or valances.

The order was larger than at first sight appears. Each set was to consist of four curtains 8 to 9 feet deep, two of which were to be $1\frac{1}{2}$ yards wide and the other pair $3\frac{1}{2}$ yards wide, 'with Tester and Head-piece proporconable', and valances 1 foot deep and $6\frac{1}{2}$ yards long. With them was to come 'a Counterpane of the same work to be $3\frac{1}{2}$ yards wide and 4 yards long, half of them to be quilted,

and the other half not quilted'; as well as 2 small carpets 1½ yards wide and 2 yards long, and 12 cushions 'of the same work'. Helpfully, but with a note of desperation, the directors added: 'By the ship you shall have variety of patterns and further directions, but be doing what you can in the meantime.' But for neither the first nor the last time the English merchants failed to keep pace with their continental competitors in this important matter, and before long the factors were moved to complain that if only the directors would send them regular supplies of patterns, it would be greatly to everybody's advantage. The Dutch and French were, they indicated, much more punctual in attending to this side of the business.

With her painted hangings replaced by Indian palampores, the embroiderer's interest in her crewel work curtains and their all-over coiling patterns worked in monochromatic colours was bound to wane. How old fashioned they must have looked beside the new light weight cottons that were prettily coloured, washable and fast dyed. No wonder she diverted her energies, her twill weave fabric, and her crewel wools to working the new designs.

Apes for Imitation

The English factory at Surat consisted of an extensive complex of warehouses, offices, living quarters for the staff, a suite for the president, a council chamber, a chapel, and a Turkish bath. The salaries of the Company's employees were not high but the opportunities for entering into private trading agreements with the local traders or *banyans* were endless. Those who piled up fortunes in this way were called *nabobs* after the Mughul governors.

Life in the factory ran on well organised lines. The day began with prayers at six o'clock followed by breakfast, after which the *banyans* invaded the compound until midday when a light luncheon was served. Book work occupied most of the afternoon and the gates of the factory were locked at nine. On Sundays the staff repaired to a garden outside the city where they could enjoy *al fresco* meals and swim in the large tank. The cooks were mostly English or Portuguese and the table wines imported from Spain or Persia. In addition the English learnt to drink a concoction made from five ingredients—brandy, lime, sugar, spice, and hot water—which they called *punch* after the Hindustani word for five.

In spite of the heat the English continued upon all formal occasions to wear their ordinary, heavy and close fitting clothes. The ambassador's chaplain, Edward Terry, never went outside without putting on his long, black, woollen cassock. Looking back in after years he realised what figures of fun he and his companions must have cut to the Indians. In his diary, which he published in 1665 as *A Voyage to the East Indies*, he wrote: 'The Colours and Fashion of our Garments are so different from their's, that we need not, wheresoever we are, to invite spectators to take notice of us.' Excellent tailors, and blessed with extraordinarily skill in making a replica of anything they were shown, the Indians quickly learnt to make clothes for the Englishmen when those they brought with them wore out.

> The Indians are the best Apes for Imitation in all the world [Terry wrote]; so full of ingenuity that they can make any new thing by pattern, how hard soever it seemeth to be done, and therefore it is no marvel that they can make these Shoes and Boots, Clothes and Linnen, and Bands and Cuffs of our English Fashion, which are all of them very different from their own Fashions and Habits, yet they make them exceedingly neatly.

33 Fragment of a late seventeenth century hanging related to the palampore in illustration 35.

A contemporary of Terry's, a Frenchman named Francois Bernier, who travelled in India between 1656 and 1668, has left us a description of the *kar-kanays* or palace workrooms of the Mughul emperors.

> In one hall embroiderers are busily employed, superintended by a master. In another you see the goldsmiths; in a third, the painters; in a fourth, varnishers in lacquer-work; in a fifth, joiners, turners, tailors and shoe-makers; in a sixth, manufacturers of silk, brocade and fine muslins.

Every morning the workers repaired to their respective *kar-kanays* where they remained until evening. Nobody sought to better himself, and nobody moved from one craft to another. 'The embroiderer brings up his son as an embroiderer,' Bernier wrote, 'the son of a goldsmith becomes a goldsmith, and the physician of the city educates his son for a physician. No one marries but in their own trade or profession.' The textile painter, we may assume, also brought up his son to be a textile painter—that is, a maker of palampores, pintadoes, or chintz.

Long ago these clever craftsmen had discovered that if they added certain natural substances to their dyes, they acted as fixatives or mordants rendering their colours completely fast. What, in effect, they did was to make the colour adhere not only to the outside of the cotton fibres, but to penetrate each one and suffuse it with colour. No European dyers had ever succeeded in doing this; nor was the woad from which they made blue dye naturally fast like the Indians' indigo, with the result that indigo became one of the East India Company's most lucrative imports. Nevertheless many years were to elapse before a systematic attempt was made to investigate the nature of the mordants that made the colours on the palampores not only impervious to strong light but also to frequent washing.

Opposite and above: drawings relating to illustration 34 (overleaf).

opposite

34 *Hanging from a set of which one, now in the Royal Ontario Museum, Toronto, bears the date 1696.*

overleaf

35 *The Ashburnham Hanging. Painted and dyed palampore made in India for the European market during the late seventeenth or early eighteenth century. There are recognisably English flowers—carnations, marigolds, and roses, as well as Indianised versions of the iris, corn-flower, and honeysuckle. See also illustration 33.*

overleaf

36 Part of a palampore made in India for the European market during the first part of the eighteenth century. Plainly the Indian draughtsman has never seen a nosegay tied with a ribbon bow. For detail see illustration 50.

opposite

37 Hanging, early eighteenth century. Heraldic lion, cockatrice, and griffin in curious juxtaposition with a parakeet and two rabbits. Originally worked on cotton twill and later remounted on linen.

Towards the middle of the eighteenth century a French Jesuit missionary working in Pondicherry, named Father Coeurdoux, found that among the members of a class he was preparing for baptism was a group of textile painters, and began to question them about their work. From their replies and such observations as he himself was able to make, he estimated that at least twenty six processes were involved in printing each palampore. In 1742 he wrote to a colleague in France describing the elaborate ritual of washings, soakings, dryings, bleachings, and beatings that had to be followed meticulously in order to prepare the cotton to receive the mordants and dyes and to render the surface so smoothly polished that nothing would hinder the movement of the painter's brush across it. He described in detail the Indians' method of transferring the design in these words

> Our native workmen use nothing beyond the pounce of the embroiderers. The painter, having carefully made his design upon the paper, pricks the outlines of it with a very fine needle, then lays the paper upon the cloth and passes over it the pounce [a little bag of charcoal powder], which penetrates through the pricked holes, and by this means the design is transferred to the cloth. With a brush or pencil he then touches up the outlines.

Then, quite suddenly, in the middle of his accurate reporting, Father Coeurdoux takes us out under the blazing Indian sky and shows us the wax being spread over the parts of the design that are to resist the dye; how the cloth is spread out in the burning sun for a few minutes to allow the wax to melt sufficiently to penetrate through to the other side; how it is then withdrawn, turned over, and pressed inch by inch by hand over the smooth bottom of an inverted bowl to ensure that every bit is evenly protected, before being passed on to the indigo dyer, a man with so highly developed a sense of smell that he can detect the second at which the dye has reached the right stage of fermentation for the cloth to be submerged in it. The madder dye, unlike the indigo, was easily handled. 'It is usually children who paint the red,' Father Coeurdoux wrote, 'because this work is less laborious. Notwithstanding,' he added, 'one could not wish for more perfect work.' The brushes they used were made from a stick of bamboo 'shaped and split at one end for the distance of one finger breadth' into which a scrap of rag was forced. This mop was then dipped into the madder and any surplus moisture squeezed out between the fingers.

The twentieth century embroiderer, accustomed to making her own designs, has no difficulty in understanding what happened when the Indian draughtsmen tried to copy the patterns sent out from England. She knows how very different the final draft of her design will be from her first rough sketch; how impossible it is to recapture its impetuous spontaneity; how each time she re-draws it, the design moves a little further away from the original; and how, when she eventually enlarges it, it changes once again, perhaps revealing an inherent weakness she has not noticed in the earlier versions. So she will not be surprised that in re-drawing the patterns given to them by the factors, and probably altering them to fill given dimensions, as in the order for the hundred sets of bed furnishings, the Indian textile painter should have changed them. For what could he know

38 A European traveller in India painted by a Mughul artist in the latter part of the sixteenth century.

about the motifs currently being used by English designers? That he copied them as successfully as he did was no doubt due largely to his special facility, noted by Edward Terry, as an imitator. But it is one thing for a craftsman to unpick a doublet or a pair of shoes and make a replica of them, and quite another to copy a design embodying motifs so far removed from his own experience as an English shepherd, a rabbit, a fox, or a nosegay of English flowers tied up with a pretty ribbon bow. How little the Indian draughtsman understood what he was drawing is clearly shown in the palampores in illustrations 35 and 36.

But for the embroiderer the most important change he made was probably in his rendering of the oak leaves that are such a feature of her crewel work. How he must have puzzled over the branches with their big baroque leaves like those on the Hatton Garden hangings [40]. Unconsciously, as he copied them, he added something of his essential 'Indian-ness', making them less realistic, and decorating them with small repeating patterns and naturalistic motifs, many of which he in turn had borrowed from Islamic art. For if the early palampores were unacceptable to the English, the art of India had appeared equally crude and unprepossessing to the Mughul emperors when they rose to power during the sixteenth century. Quickly they summoned Persian miniature painters to their court and, by the time that Jahangir, the fourth of the line, had come to the throne, a style that was neither Indian nor Persian but was recognisably Mughul had emerged from a synthesis between them. It was onto this style that the patterns sent out from England were grafted, and whose influence can therefore be plainly seen on English crewel work.

To appreciate why the English, in common with all other Europeans, should not have known that there was any difference between the art of India and the art of China is not difficult. It is perhaps not quite so obvious why, when they had never visited China, they should have been so convinced they knew what it was like.

In the middle ages men believed that beyond India there was a range of mountains so high that the waters of the Flood had not covered them, and that beyond lay a Paradise Garden that they called Cathay. Gazing in delighted enchantment at the patterns on the luminous silks and translucent ceramics that occasionally reached the west, they speculated about what it was like. One thing leading to another, it was not very long before they convinced themselves that they knew. Nourishing their imagination on travellers' tales, they went on adding to their dreams. Out of them they fashioned a quiet, poetic landscape, where trees grew out of gently rounded blue hills or from rocks whose carefully contrived canyons and perforations seemed to owe more to art than nature. The branches of the trees, by some strange magic, bore at the same time—like the trees in the Garden of Eden—all manner of leaves, fruit, and flowers; and afforded shelter to fascinatingly decorative birds with long, undulating necks, wide-spread wings, and spectacularly sweeping tails.

By the beginning of the sixteenth century an embroiderer named Mary Hulton was embroidering in canvas work a pattern [41] that reflected the influence of Cathay, the country that never was. At first glance it looks typically renaissance in style. There is a central shield surmounted by a Tudor rose, and supported by two diminutive white dogs, and two identical golden lions— the stock in trade of every English embroiderer. The border, too, is no more than

39 One of a set of ten canvas work panels completed by Lady Julia Calverley in 1716 for her home at Esholt Hall, Northumberland. Now at Wallington, Northumberland.

40 One of a set of six canvas work panels from a house in Hatton Garden, London, embroidered in tent, brick, cross, and rococo stitches with couching and French knots. Made during the second half of the seventeenth century.

41 Long cushion cover signed 'Mary Hulton' and worked during the reign of James I.

a regular repeating pattern, though the twentieth century embroiderer will be quick to notice that Mary Hulton, like all her contemporaries, attached little importance to making it turn the corner properly. But surely the hillock and the matching pair of branches growing out of it are something new in English embroidery? Where did the pattern drawer find this pointed blue mountain covered with small rounded foothills? and where did he get these triple rooted yet rootless trees, these branches on which bunches of grapes and such essentially English flowers as honeysuckle, marigolds, and carnations flourish side by side with many-petalled flowers to which it is difficult to put a name and which seem to be best described as exotic? Surely such romantic and magical things could only happen in the remote and beautiful land of Cathay. Probably they are not so very different from some at least of the patterns sent out to the factors by the directors of the East India Company, but small wonder they saw nothing in them to remind them of Chinese art. Busily they set to work to produce them on their painted cottons not only for the English merchants, but also for export to China. The Chinese were delighted with them, imagining them to be something new and different in the way of textile design.

The elusive Abigail Pett

In 1664 a lady of the Verney family began working what she described as 'a dimity curtain in gren cruells'. As many people know to their cost, she was by no means the last embroiderer to embark upon a project that was too ambitious and who, when she began to weary of it, complained about the pattern

> There is too much work in it and there is certain birds and flyes and other creepers which I do not know, and frutes that I do not like . . . but it is a very fine thing though they be left out.

42 Roundel from the back of the work bag in illustration 46.

43 *Two of a set of four bed curtains signed Abigail Pett and worked in greens, dark blues, yellows, and browns, with touches of emerald and carmine. The valances have a single row of large detached leaves.*

opposite
44 *An eighteenth century bed, Blickling Hall, Norfolk. Compare with illustration 43.*

No such disenchantment seems to have overtaken Abigail Pett whose bed hangings and valances, as much because the embroiderer's name can be attached to them as for the sake of the easily copied detached motifs that constitute the design, have exerted such a wide influence upon twentieth century crewel work [43]. How good it would be, therefore, if we knew who she was.

The Petts were a seafaring family and the Admiralty records for the seventeenth century list no less than eleven named Phineas and sixteen called Peter. Abigail, too, was a popular girl's name at a time when people studied the Old Testament and knew well the story of Abigail, the wife of Nabal 'a woman of good understanding and beautiful countenance' who, when her husband churlishly refused the young men sent to him by David to ask for food and drink, set out herself, loaded with provisions, to prevent David from taking justifiable revenge upon him; and who, when next day she told Nabal what she had done, causing him to suffer a stroke from which ten days later he died, became the wife of David and therefore an ancestor of Christ.

One of the Peter Petts was a Master shipbuilder and was known to both John Evelyn and Samuel Pepys. He supported the Parliamentary party during the Civil War and, presumably in recognition of his services, was made Commissioner of the Chatham dockyard. On Sunday 3 August 1662, Pepys visited him at Chatham and noted in his diary

44 A pair of crewel embroidered shoes of the 1730s.

Drawings relating to illustration 46.

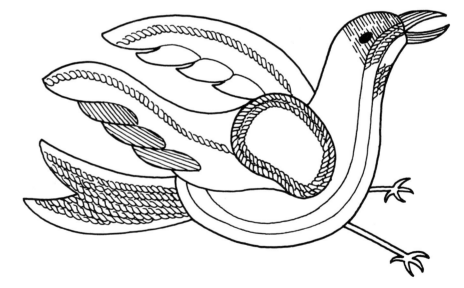

opposite
46 Work bag embroidered in 1747 with detached motifs in chain, closed herringbone, coral, and long and short stitches, with bullion knots. For the roundel on the back see illustration 42.

overleaf
47, 48 Work bag signed 'E.M.' and dated 1699, mainly in stem, back, and satin stitches. The drawstrings, tassels, and fringe are original.

49 *Crewel work comes under the influence of the eighteenth century taste for naturalism and the gently undulating line of the rococo.*

> Up early and with Captain Cocke to the Dockyard . . . where we walked till Commissioner Pett came and took us to his house and showed us his garden and fine things, and gave us a fine breakfast of bread and butter and sweetmeats and other things, with great choice of strong drinks which I could not avoid making my head ache, tho' I drank but little.

Mrs Pett it seems, was a good housewife and kept a lavish table. They then went by coach to church and listened to a dull sermon, and later Pett showed them his collection of curiosities, including some fine model ships. The following summer Evelyn, too, visited Pett and also saw his models. He described the house as being like a Roman villa surrounded by a pretty garden and furnished with urns, statues, and cypress trees.

But in June 1667 when the Dutch admiral, de Ruyter, sailed unhindered up the Medway, sank a number of naval vessels, and towed away the *Royal Charles*, flagship of the English fleet, Peter Pett was the obvious scapegoat. He was dismissed from his post and retired into obscurity in Norfolk. Probably he had spent too much time on his house and garden and too little in the dockyard. Pepys seems to have distrusted him as 'a weak and silly man that is guilty of horrid neglect in the business all along'. But he sympathised with him in the loss of his garden. 'I must confess,' he wrote, 'it must need be a sorrowful thing for a man that hath taken so much pain to make a place neat.' Pett himself regretted the loss of his garden ornaments, his sundial, statues, and urns which the authorities refused to send on to him.

Unfortunately none of Peter Pett's daughters was called Abigail, nor is there any record of a child of that name having been baptised in St Mary's, Chatham, where Pepys heard the dull sermon. He did, however, have an aunt called Abigail.

Peter Pett's father, one of the many Phineas Petts, was one of a family of twelve. From Phineas's autobiography, which was published by the Naval Records Society in 1894, we learn that his mother, having been widowed at an early age, married a clergyman named Thomas Nunn, taking with her to her new home two of her daughters, one of whom was called Abigail. Shortly afterwards she died.

Apparently Thomas Nunn was a man of ungovernable temper, and in a moment of violent rage battered Abigail to death. Phineas described the ghastly scene in these words.

> Upon a slight occasion about making clean his cloak being wet and dirty with riding a journey the day before, he fell furiously upon my eldest sister Abigail, beating her so cruelly with a pair of tongs and a firebrand that she died within a few days.

Unfortunately this shocking episode occurred in 1599, many years before any embroiderer began working patterns even remotely similar to those on the hangings signed by the elusive Abigail Pett. However, all the above information at least gives an indication of the areas in which research is being concentrated. Meanwhile the identity of this talented embroiderer remains a mystery.

Pretty, wayward and romantic

If the seventeenth century lady as depicted on the title page of *The Needle's Excellency* [11], and described by Mrs Evelyn and Gervase Markham, was to be a model of all the domestic virtues, the eighteenth century lady—while not neglecting the duties Swift expected her to perform—was prepared to find life amusing and enjoyable. She dressed herself in mantuas made of rustling taffeta and shimmering satin, over petticoats embroidered in an ecstacy of flowery patterns, and decorated with laces, bows, and flounces. Heavily ornate furniture disappeared and was replaced by chairs and tables of elegant proportions with inlaid patterns and gilded rococo ornament. Out of the fantasy world of Cathay came the delicious style we call chinoiserie. At its heart lay the stately pleasure domes, the caverns measureless to man, and the

> . . . gardens bright with sinuous rills,
> Where blossomed many an incense-bearing tree

evoked by Coleridge in the poem he created out of his dream about Xanadu, the remote, magical city of Kublai Khan and Marco Polo. It was the day of the porcelain figurines made at Chelsea and Bow, the furniture of Thomas Chippendale, the pagoda at Kew, and the beautiful flowing movements of the minuet.

From being forceful and assertive the patterns of crewel work became pretty, wayward, and romantic. Thick branches disappeared and were succeeded by meandering stems and delectable swags and nosegays of flowers tied with long, fluttering ribbons. Leaves formerly big, bold, and flamboyant, became narrow and flattened. Where once they had curled over with splended three-dimensional effect, the edges now rippled along as if trimmed with scraps of lace or braid. The more the embroiderer refined her work, the smaller and more delicate became the motifs, the larger the spaces between them, and the less obtrusive her stitches. It was as though exhausted by such an abundance of crewel work she had to bring embroidery back into scale with the needle and thread. Whether

50 Detail of a bird from the palampore in illustration 36.

she worked a pattern in silk or crewels her object was the same—to shade it to perfection [49, 51, 52, 53, 57].

How much importance was attached to shading is brought out strongly by the account given by Campbell in *The London Tradesman* of the work of the professional embroiderer. It is quite astonishing to find how much significance he attaches at this early date to the need for the embroiderer to have some knowledge of the principles of drawing and shading. Embroidery, he wrote, is an ingenious art that requires

> a nice Taste in Drawing, a bold Fancy to invent new Patterns, and a clean Hand to save their work from tarnishing. Few of the workers at Present can Draw; they have their Patterns from the Pattern-Drawer, who must likewise draw the Work itself [transfer it to the fabric], which they only fill up with Gold and Silver, Silks or Worsteds, according to its Use and Nature.

The English, he feared, were far from excelling at this art, falling short of the standard set by French and Italian embroiderers.

> This I take to be a want of Taste for Drawing in the Performers; they may go on in a dull beaten Tract or servily imitate a Foreign Pattern, but know not how to advance the Beauty of the old or strike out any new Invention worth Notice. An Embroiderer ought to have a Taste for Designing, and a just Notion of the Principles of Light and Shade, to know how to arrange their colours in a natural order, make them reflect upon one another, and the whole to represent the Figure in its proper shade.

The workroom manager might neglect his duty to see that his apprentices learnt to draw, but by the mid-century there can hardly have been a teacher in either England or America who did not at some time advertise her ability to teach young ladies the new and fashionable art of shading in silks and crewel wools. The patterns of crewel work had, by this time, crossed the Atlantic and the great American tradition of embroidery in crewel wools had begun. In due course the embroiderers were to develop their own recognisably national patterns and way of working.

More frank and obvious than the subtle shading of long and short stitch was the semi-striped effect the eighteenth century embroiderer created with chain stitch. Her predilection for it probably stems from the beautiful Indian silk embroideries which, unlike the palampores, had been from the earliest years one of the East India Company's more successful imports. The Hardwick inventory of 1603 shows that the Countess of Shrewsbury possessed one of their embroidered quilts. It was kept in the Wardrobe near the Pearl Bedroom (now the Blue Bedroom) and was described as: 'a quylt of yellowe india stuffe imbrodered with birdes and beastes and white silke frenge and tassells, lyned with yellowe sarcenet.'

From time immemorial the Indians, Chinese, and Mohammedans had been famous for their embroideries. Almost entirely professional, the workers tended to use a more limited range of stitches, chiefly satin and chain stitch, than those on which the English domestic embroiderer could afford to spend so many pleasurable hours. Marco Polo who, on his outward journey to China passed through the

Kingdom of Kerman, noticed that the women produced excellent silk embroidered hangings, cushion covers, and quilts worked 'with figures of beasts and birds, trees and flowers, and a variety of other patterns'. And when on the homeward voyage his ship stopped on the west coast of India, he observed that in the Kingdom of Gurjarat the embroiderers worked similar motifs in gold and silver thread on leather, making in this manner what he described as 'marvellously beautiful things' which, good merchant as he was, he estimated to be worth from six to ten silver marks.

Edward Terry, too, commented on the Indian embroiderers noting that they made

> excellent quylts of their stayn'd Cloth or fresh coloured Taffata lyned with their Pintadoes, or of Satten lyned with Taffata, betwixt which they put Cotton-Wool, and work them together with Silk.

Impressed by the extreme neatness of the stitchery, he added

> These Taffata Satten quylts are so excellently stitched by them, being done so evenly, and in as good order, as if they had been drawn out for them, for their direction, the better to work them.

He did not, however, remark on the fact that the Indians did not frame up their material, but as J. C. Irwin and Babette Hannish showed in an article published by the Needle and Bobbin Club (vol. 53, 1970) they hooked their way around the patterns holding the material in their hands.

By the eighteenth century three haberdashers, Sibella Lloyd, Martha Williams, and Elizabeth Storey, kept both satin and calico quilts, and India and French quilting. Many others were offering to draw 'India patterns' for their customers, and chain stitch embroidered chintz had become fashionable wear for ladies like Mrs Purefoy, who lived with her son Henry at Shalstone on the border between Buckinghamshire, Bedfordshire, and Northamptonshire. We have Mrs Purefoy's own word for it that she was 'a woman of excellent understanding, prudent and frugal', for these were the words she chose for the stonemason in Buckingham to carve on the monument in Shalstone church that she had erected during her lifetime. It cost her ninety-five pounds.

Henry was a sedate, priggish young man, said to 'converse more with books than men' and took his solid, well regulated life very seriously indeed. Neither he nor his mother ever sent a letter without first writing it out in draft. Fortunately for posterity their letter books for the years 1735 to 1753 have been preserved. They are as crammed with tiny scraps of information about life in a well-to-do country household in the eighteenth century as a Baccarat paperweight is of minute splinters of coloured glass. So when Mrs Purefoy decided to buy and equip one of the new-fashioned low beds, we can follow the solemn purposefulness with which Henry set about buying the 45 yards of quilting at 10s 6d a yard that she required. The correspondence was carried on as usual with Mr Anthony Baxter of Henrietta Street, Covent Garden, and a rare time he had with them.

But apparently Mrs Purefoy also fancied a length of the new chain stitch embroidered chintz to make a gown, and so on 10 February 1735, Henry wrote to

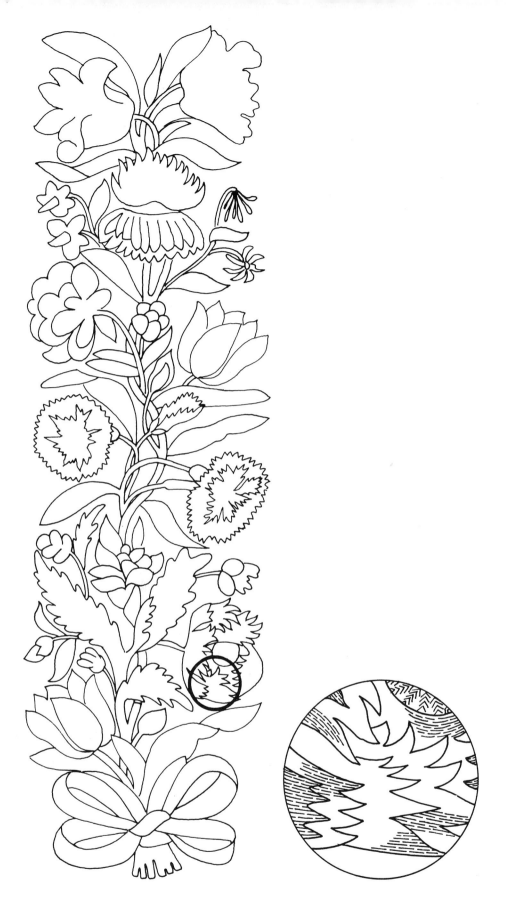

51 Eighteenth century panel with tulips, carnations, irises, and a crown imperial.

52 A remnant of eighteenth century crewel work. See illustration 57 for another example.

Mr Baxter and asked him to find 'a workt chintz' for a gown and petticoat or failing that, enough for a wrapper. Ever ready to find fault with others, Henry on this occasion made a mistake. One hopes it caused Mr Baxter some joy. Probably hearing only imperfectly what his mother said, he described the material as 'generally workt in fine *charge* stitch'!

Four prima donnas

With the eighteenth century came a revival of interest in old master paintings. The desire to foster a national school of art and to arouse public interest in works of art led to the founding of the Royal Academy of Arts, foreshadowed in a scheme proposed by John Evelyn in 1662. Its charter provided for the setting up of Schools of Design, professorships of painting, sculpture, architecture, perspective, and geometry, an annual exhibition open to all artists of distinction, the establishment of a library, and a collection of prints and drawings of classical subjects likely to be of use to students. Soon Johann Zoffany was painting his well known picture of a Members' Meeting in the life room with the proud title *The Academicians of the Royal Academy*, and before long there were not only historical and antiquarian societies all over England, but also art societies, drawing schools, and exhibitions. The interest in topographical drawing that made the designers of the Bayeux Tapestry fill up the background with pictures of churches, castles, cottages, and familiar landmarks, now took the form of landscape painting. Ladies as well as gentlemen took up sketching and attended painting classes where, like the students in the Academy Schools, they applied themselves diligently to copying famous paintings. This being so, it could only be a matter of time before the embroiderer discovered that she too could participate in this fascinating experience and take up needle painting, with the object of so perfectly imitating a picture in needlework as to trick the observer into mistaking it for the original. They found that by far and away the best thread for reproducing the marks of the master's brush was crewel wool.

Needle painting was a high and hallowed art, complete mastery of which was given only to the few; and although many must have tried their hands at it, they quickly discovered that it was too exacting a skill for them, and went back to the easier method of embroidering pretty pictures on the finest of silks and satins in smooth, shimmering silken stitchery. But it was needle painting that interested the gentlemen, and to one of them we owe a long and complete dissertation on the needle paintings of Miss Morret of Rokeby in Yorkshire.

53 The light, wandering line of the rococo set with delicate flowery sprays and small veined leaves.

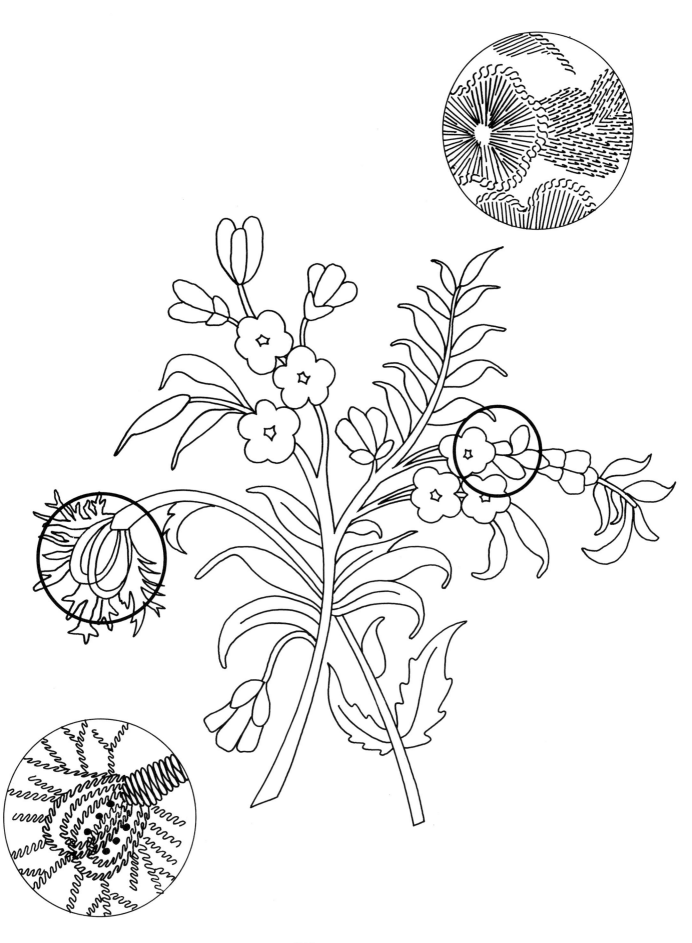

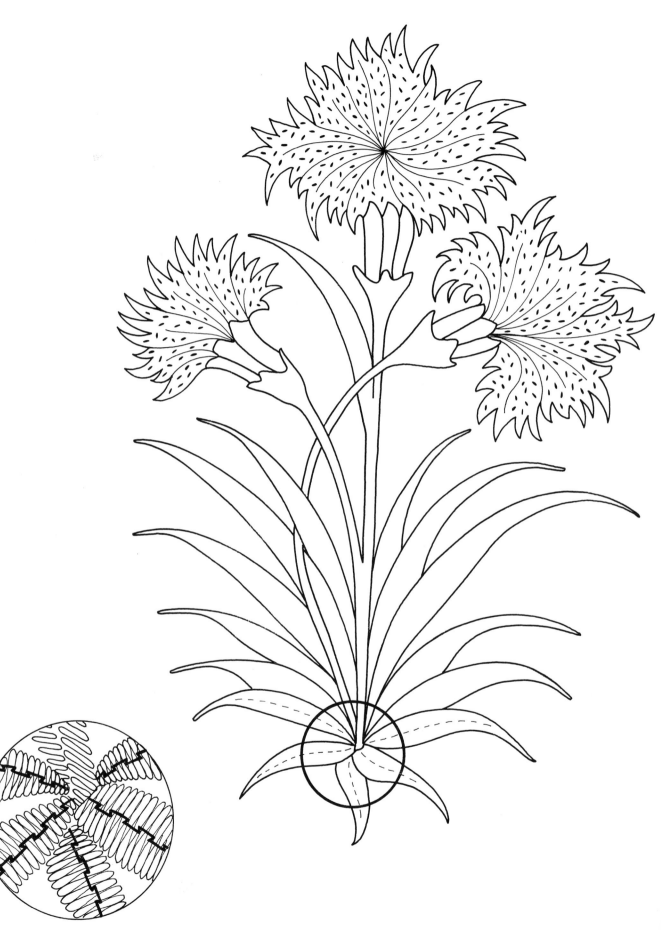

Arthur Young travelled through the northern counties of England investigating the state of the population, agriculture, and manufacture, and published the facts and figures he collected in 1771. Interspersed with them are lively descriptions of the more notable buildings in the towns he visited and of such country houses as were open to the public. In York he saw the cathedral, the castle, and the assembly rooms, went to the races, and walked beside the river; but the sight that caught his eye was, he wrote, 'the copies of several capital paintings worked by Miss Morret, a lady of most surprising genius'. Fine tapestries he claims to have seen in plenty on his travels, even an occasional bunch of grapes and a spray of flowers embroidered in a most pleasing manner, but he thought to copy oil paintings containing several figures, with a grace, a brilliancy and an elegance superior to the originals could be reserved only for the most talented ladies. So impressed was he with Miss Morret's *tour de force* that he proceeded to describe each one in detail. They included two landscapes by Zuccarelli, two by Gaspar Poussin, an unfinished work after Rubens, and one by Salvator Rosa entitled *Democritus in a Contemplative Mood* over which he waxed so enthusiastic that the reader might suppose Miss Morret had arranged the composition herself. He wrote

> Nothing can be more nobly designed, or more expressively finished than the figure of Democritus: his attitude is admirable, the lean of the head on the hand fine, and the light falling across the face in the most picturesque manner; nor can anything exceed the expression of the face, hands and feet.

In conclusion, Young assures those who read his comments that should the opportunity to view these most elegant productions come their way, they will find that they greatly exceed their expectations, abounding as they do 'with beauty of a most surprising and pleasing nature'.

Ten years later Mrs Lybbe Powys of Hardwick Hall in Oxfordshire set out to visit her relations in Norwich. She was accompanied by her eldest daughter Caroline and her maid Triphosa. They stayed with her cousin Mr Slaney who very properly took her to view the city and hall and the castle, which at the time was being used as the county goal. Briskly she comments that it commands a noble view of the city and country round, its thirty-six churches, and the light, elegant spire of the cathedral. In the evenings they walked in the tea gardens and on Friday visited the cathedral itself, where they admired a new stained glass window, and inquired about the pictures embroidered by the Dean's wife, Mrs Lloyd who, before her marriage, had been—so Mrs Powys noted in her diary— 'Miss Grey, the celebrated worker in worsted'. Mrs Powys was a lady who liked to have her way and by Sunday morning she had prevailled upon Mrs Green, 'the clergyman's lady', to take her to the Deanery to see Mrs Lloyd's work. Less ecstatic than Arthur Young, she was undoubtedly impressed by 'the quite amazing pictures' with which she was confronted. The portrait of a hermit holding a folio prayer book is 'beyond description' she wrote, but could not decide whether one of an old gardener in his stall with a young girl was not even superior.

Another famous exponent of the art was Mrs Mary Knowles, the daughter of two prominent Quakers of Rugeley in Staffordshire named Moses and Mary Morris. She was a beautiful, witty and accomplished woman who, when on a visit to France with her husband, a noted London physician, was received at Versailles and had the honour of being admitted to the *toilette* of Marie Antoinette. When examples of her work were shown to George III and Queen Charlotte they were so delighted with them that she was summoned to court and commissioned to embroider the portrait of the king painted by Johann Zoffany in 1771. Overjoyed with this mark of royal favour she subsequently set about embroidering a picture of herself at work on the Zoffany portrait!

A noted conversationalist, Mrs Knowles was a welcome addition to any dinner party, and on more than one occasion was present when Dr Johnson and James Boswell were among the guests. She and Johnson first met at a small dinner party given by a famous bookseller, Mr Dilly. In a letter written to his friend Mrs Thrale on 16 May 1776, Johnson told her of the event, identifying Mrs Knowles for her as a lady who worked 'sutile pictures in needlework'. How the mistake occurred has never been satisfactorily explained, but when the correspondence between Johnson and Mrs Thrale was published, it was found that a cross bar had been added to Johnson's long 'S', perhaps by the printer himself or an over-zealous proof reader, and the word appeared as 'futile', giving the impression that Johnson had no great opinion of needle painting. The matter was only cleared up in 1788 when, as the result of a wager, somebody turned up the original letter.

On Wednesday 15 April 1778, Johnson and Mrs Knowles were again at Mr Dilly's. It was the celebrated occasion on which Johnson, reluctant to put down the book he had been reading when dinner was announced, kept it wrapped up in the table cloth on his knee throughout the meal, resembling, as Boswell was quick to notice, 'a dog that holds a bone in his paws, while he eats something else that has been thrown to him'. He was pleased at the quickness with which Mrs Knowles capped this apt remark: 'He knows how to read a book better than anyone; he gets at the substance of the book directly; he tears the heart out of it.'

Later Mrs Knowles affected to complain because men had much more liberty allowed them than women, and Boswell faithfully reported Johnson as replying

> Why, Madam, women have all the liberty they should wish to have. We have all the labour and the danger, and the women all the advantage. We go to sea, we build houses, we do everything, in short to pay our court to the women.

But Mrs Knowles was not to be persuaded. 'I hope', she remarked austerly, 'that in another world the sexes will be equal.'

Finally, there was Miss Mary Linwood, the best remembered needle painter of them all. She was born at Birmingham in 1755, just six years before Marie Grosholtz, whom the world knows as Madame Tussaud. Both ladies succeeded in making their exhibitions a popular feature of London life; but unlike Marie Tussaud's waxworks, interest in Mary Linwood's needle paintings died with her.

54 A wool portrait of George III by Mrs Mary Knowles.

She enjoys, however, the unique distinction of having maintained an exhibition of embroidery in London for so long a period that it became a regular tourist attraction, finding a place for itself in such publications as *Mogg's New Picture of London and Visitors' Guide to its Sights*, in which the writer observed

> This beautiful style of needlework is the invention of a Leicestershire lady, and consists of 59 copies of the finest pictures in the English and foreign schools of art, possessing all the correct drawing, just colouring, and light and shade of the original pictures from which they are taken; in a word, Miss Linwood's exhibition is one of the most beautiful the metropolis can boast and should unquestionably be witnessed, as it deserves to be, by every admirer of art.

The exhibition is also mentioned in a somewhat grander contemporary guide book called *Curiosities of London*, which was compiled by a Fellow of the Society of Antiquaries named Horace Welby who wrote under the pseudonym Dr John Timbs. Miss Linwood appears among the famous personages who at one time or another occupied houses in Leicester Square. There was Leicester House itself, where George III had been proclaimed king and Sir Ashton Lever exhibited his collection of curiosities, and the house where Hogarth spent the last ten years of his life. Next door Dr John Hunter kept his anatomical collection and on Sunday evenings held his medical levees, and on the opposite side, at no. 47, Sir Joshua Reynolds entertained such distinguished company as Dr Johnson, Garrick, and Goldsmith. Beside Leicester House stood Savile House, the property of the Earl of Aylesbury. Into it, in 1809, moved Mary Linwood and her needlework paintings. The exhibition was to remain open until her death in 1845.

Perhaps it was just as well that Reynolds was already dead. Imitation may be the sincerest form of flattery, but whether he would have viewed with unalloyed pleasure the prospect of living cheek by jowl with four of his paintings in crewel wools is debatable. As President of the Royal Academy he can hardly have been unaware of Miss Linwood's attempts to get her work hung in its exhibitions, and of the hanging committee's steadfast refusal to have anything to do with them. But she was not without other honours. In 1786 she was awarded a medal by the Society for the Encouragement of the Arts for her 'excellent imitations of pictures in needlework'; and in the same year was summoned to court where, according to the *Morning Post*, she had the honour of exhibiting to their Majesties 'several pieces of needlework wrought in a style superior to anything of the kind yet attempted', for which she received the Queen's 'highest encomiums'. But although no commission such as Mrs Knowles received was forthcoming, other royal personages fell victims to the spell. The Empress of Russia was pleased to accept an example of her work, and the King of Poland was among her most fervent admirers; while Napoleon, whose portrait she embroidered twice, is reported to have tried to persuade her to bring her exhibition to Paris.

But Mary Linwood's exhibition was not easily transportable. Not for her the walls hung with embroidered panels that can be taken down, packed up,

55 Mary Linwood's portrait of Napoleon completed in 1825.

and rehung somewhere else tomorrow. First at the Panthenon in Oxford Street, then briefly at the Hanover Square Concert Rooms, and finally in Savile House, she arranged each item in its appropriate and carefully planned setting. Like Madame Tussaud, she made a kind of peep-show, a series of specially designed scenes, at the centre of which she placed one of her needle paintings. She had discovered a fascinating if child-like game in which she could play all the parts herself: she was entrepreneur, the stage manager, stage designer, lighting expert (she was the first gallery proprietor to install gas lighting in order to keep open on winter afternoons), and above all the leading lady. It is perhaps unkind, but true, to suggest that her most successful role was probably that of publicity officer. She was unique and she knew it. She had come a long way since, as a young girl, she had exhibited a specimen of her work with the Society of Artists in Leicester. Now, with theatrical panache, she hung her main gallery with scarlet and silver, and admitted the public to admire the spectacles she created.

They came in their hundreds. Here, in a gloomy prison cell, was her copy of James Northcote's historical painting of *Lady Jane Grey visited by the Abbot and Keeper of the Tower by Night*. From a carefully contrived and rocky cave, the spectator caught sight of a brilliantly lit sunny seascape beyond. There was Raphael's *Madonna della Sedia*, three landscapes by Joseph Wright of Derby, and by 1820 no less than six copies of paintings by George Morland, each suitably enshrined. George Stubbs was another of her favourites, and she exhibited her version of his lioness in a bone-strewn cavern of such astonishing reality that the editor of the *Ladies' Magazine* was moved to describe it as having all the effect of nature itself

> the situation of the animal in its den being so forcible and appropriate that the mind suffers for a moment the awful impression of the creature being alive and ready to attack any intruder upon her solitude.

The picture to which she herself was most firmly attached and which she ultimately left in her will to Queen Victoria, was her rendering of the over-smooth and sentimental picture, *Salvator Mundi*, by the seventeenth century Italian artist Carlo Dolci, the impact of which was calculated to bring the properly atuned viewers to their knees as, clutching their catalogues, they got their reactions right by reading the stirring lines

> Who climb with sober awe, in thought aspires,
> Catches pure zeal, and, as he gazes, fires;
> Feels a new ardour to his sould convey'd,
> Submissive bows, and venerates the shade.

Never were crewel wools put to stranger use.

Naturally the exhibition included John Hoppner's portrait of Miss Linwood which is now in the Victoria and Albert Museum. There she sits, perpetually pretty and girlish, surrounded by a flurry of wool, the work on which she is

56 A portrait of Mary Linwood by Richard Westall, 1799.

57 Another example of eighteenth century crewel work. See also illustration 52.

58 The central portion of a hanging designed by William Morris.

engaged not lying horizontally like an ordinary embroidery frame, but reared up before her like an artist's easel. But then was she not an artist, a painter, albeit not with the brush but with the needle? Richard Westall surely thought so [56].

Mary Linwood was not creative—she was not a designer. Although it is said that she herself outlined her pictures on the specially woven tammy cloth on which she preferred to work, only three out of the hundred paintings listed in the 1820 catalogue are original works. There is one called *Fox alarmed, Stealing from Shelter*, and two landscapes, one of which has no title and the other is called *A Fishing Party*. All the rest are copies.

Of course it could not last. Sooner or later the bubble had to burst, the dream had to end. Once the leading lady had taken her last curtain calls and bowed herself out, the gas lights went out, and the show was over. After her death when her pictures were sold, it was discovered that it had been the spectacle not the embroidery that the crowds had come to see. Separated from each other, and detached from their settings, they were almost valueless. A lot of people said they had always known this was how it would be. When the collection was offered to The Trustees of the British Museum it was declined.

There was still an epilogue to follow. In the 1820 catalogue of the exhibition there are listed four needle paintings after Thomas Gainsborough: *Children at the Fire, Girl and Cat entering the Cottage, Woodman in the Storm*, and *Shepherd's Boy in a Storm*. Because the *Woodman in the Storm* was accidently destroyed in a fire, Mary Linwood's copy is the only surviving record of it, and is therefore of considerable interest to art historians. At her death it fetched £33 15s 0d, and is in the Leicester Museum. This may be a very different kind of posthumous fame from that which Mary Linwood, like most embroiderers, dreamt of, but at least it is secure and useful. No one can ask for more.

In September 1813 an amusing letter on needle painting appeared in the *Ladies' Magazine*. The subject was 'The Industrious Housewife' and the writer signed himself Benedict. In it he holds up to ridicule the whole mystique surrounding this type of embroidery. His wife was an undoubted expert at it; in fact, he wrote, she could imitate paintings so well with her needle that the ingenuity of her performances excited universal admiration. He complains, however, that although his drawing room is adorned with her pictures, his children are frequently ragged, for their mother 'who can accomplish everything fantastic or beautiful with her needle' can neither cut out a shirt nor sew on a button. When he remonstrates with her she promises to look to these mundane matters when she has finished this or that piece of embroidery; but experience has taught him that he will only see it succeeded by another, equally expensive, elegant, and useless. 'Meantime I have the mortification', he concludes, 'to find I am esteemed a fortunate man, for having a pretty wife, always at home, and always industrious.' No doubt the gentleman was writing with his tongue in his cheek, but no embroiderer will be without her whiff of sympathy for his wife's reluctance to put down her work to attend to more pressing household tasks.

overleaf
59 Mary Linwood's needle painting of Woodman in the Storm *by Thomas Gainsborough.*

Entr'acte III

When art brought crewel work into fashion
and crewels made swifter progress than art,
many rooms were filled with pieces of linen,
hung over the furniture in such quantity as
to recall a washing day, each decorated with
a spray of brightly coloured flowers.

Elizabeth Glaister, 1880

When the Great Exhibition of 1851 closed its doors for the last time, the stands
were dismantled, and the Crystal Palace empty and hushed, a few serious-minded
men were left with a problem on their hands. Why, they asked themselves, when
England was commercially the richest nation on earth, and could play host to the
rest of the world with such unprecedented success, should it have been made so
embarrassingly plain that in matters of taste and design her manufacturers lagged
so far behind those of her foreign competitors? It was no consolation to discover
that only Belgium, the smallest country in Europe, had exhibited goods decorated
with the same unrefined and unoriginal designs.

Convinced that the only remedy lay in educating public taste, they decided to
devote a large part of the considerable profit, which contrary to all prognostica-
tions had accrued from the Exhibition, to founding a museum where people
could study the finest examples of the decorative arts, not only of Europe but also
of the Near and Far East. Known at first as the South Kensington Museum, it was
later renamed the Victoria and Albert Museum. Some of the earliest objects collected for it were examples of crewel work.

The Belgian government did not sit idly by. They sent a noted economist, the
Chevalier de Cocqueil, to England to report on the system of teaching in the
drawing schools where the nation's industrial designers were trained. He had a
sorry story to tell. He found that the teachers, being art school trained, thought the
creation of a design was one thing, and its application quite another. To adapt it

to the loom, the wheel, or the wall paper printing machine was, they believed no concern of the designer. The manufacturers on the other hand, with full order books and a complacent public, were only too happy to spend as little as possible on the decoration of their products; and far from seeking out the better designers and paying them an adequate fee, preferred to pirate designs from France and Germany, leaving the men on the factory floor to adapt them to their machines as best they could.

Crisply the Chevalier contrasted this with the situation in Lyons where designers for the great silk weaving industry were trained. Here, he reported, students were taught not only the principles of colour and design, but actually superintended the weaving of their patterns in the factories, adapting them to the looms and making any necessary changes in the colour scheme themselves. The success of the industry thus lay, he concluded, in the co-operation between the artist and the craftsman who executed his design. Regretfully he noted that as long as English manufacturers and teachers refused to accept the logic of this system, no men of talent were likely to be attracted to industrial design.

He was justified in his opinion. William Morris, the man who in the end changed the face of English design, would have nothing to say to machine-made goods. Hating their coarse lines and garish colours, he set about making things for every day use that were a pleasure to handle and a delight to the eye. In the process he gave the patterns of crewel work an entirely new twist.

William Morris and The Wood beyond the World

William Morris was born in 1834 at Walthamstow on the edge of Epping Forest. The tops of the trees can still be seen from the upper windows of the house where he was brought up, a blue green smudge in summer and a line of purple in winter. Even today when the suburban houses of north London press closely around it, it remains a strange, mysterious place, whose secret rides and hidden depths seem to have changed little since the middle ages. It was the perfect place for a boy with a natural love of beauty and an intense interest in birds and flowers to grow up. When he went away to boarding school he continued to go for long, solitary walks—a habit he was to follow throughout his life—beguiling the time by telling himself romantic tales of knights and ladies, spell binding magicians, wicked dwarfs, and fire breathing dragons. When he went up to Oxford the narrow, medieval lanes winding between the colleges, the river, the spires, and the chiming bells were like nothing so much as an extension of his dreams.

At Exeter College he met another first year student, Edward Burne-Jones. They were to remain friends throughout their lives. But beautiful as Oxford might be, it was not long before Burne-Jones decided that his true vocation lay in painting, and he departed to London; while Morris, soon abandoning his original intention of taking holy orders, entered the office of G. E. Street, one of the foremost architects of the Gothic Revival, with the idea of becoming an architect. Here he made another lasting friend, Philip Webb, whom he was later to invite to design a house for him at Bexleyheath in Kent, after his marriage to the beautiful Jane Burden. Speaking at the opening of the Morris centennial exhibition at the Victoria and Albert Museum, their younger daughter May was to recall that because her father would have nothing in his house that was not both beautiful and useful, and could find nothing in the shops except a few Persian rugs and some blue and white Delft pottery that measured up to these requirements, he set about designing them himself. Out of this grew the firm of Morris & Company. But in retrospect May Morris saw it all like some enchanted fairy tale.

These early experiments in furnishings [she said] more or less decided Morris's career as a designer and decorator; but he did not work alone. All the friends must help; the women made embroidered hangings; the men painted tiles and the furniture was designed by Philip Webb . . . Rossetti and Burne-Jones, the professional artists of the circle, painted pictures on the walls and panelling; the rooms were alive with happy workers, the garden gay with flowers . . . but the work done was serious and became tradition, laying the foundation of the Arts and Crafts Movement in England.

The designer-craftsman—the artist who, unlike the men trained in the industrial design schools, knew that before he could design for a craft he must understand its techniques—had arrived on the scene. So when Morris wanted to design hangings for Red House he sat down to teach himself the stitches of embroidery.

The reason why Morris should have preferred crewel work to any other method of embroidery is not hard to find. Neither the saints and angels nor the refined stitchery of the *opus anglicanum* suited his purpose; and canvas work was altogether too slow and too well regulated to appeal to him. But crewel work has always been associated with hangings: its patterns were big and flowing and in scale with his panelled rooms; the way its leaves curled over along the edges reminded him of those he saw in the medieval manuscripts he collected so eagerly; while the early examples of crewel work he studied in the Victoria and Albert Museum with their muted, monochromatic colours, pleased and satisfied his eye. Besides, the stitches of crewel work were mobile and decorative, and with long and short stitch he could make his crewels blend softly and sweetly into one another like the feathers on a bird's wing. Then there were its traditional materials —a plain, homely, unpretentious textile, and tough, stringy wools that a man could handle, and that were so different from the floppy, fluffy Berlin wools with their bright yellows, sharp greens, and the Prussian blue, which of all colours in the spectrum he most heartily detested.

For his original experiments Morris had some crewels specially dyed with vegetable dyes. Jane found a length of plain indigo-dyed serge, and as soon as he saw it he sat down and began at a great rate to design flowers for it. They stretched it on a frame which, scorning the fashionable lady's flimsy frame, Morris had copied from an old model, and together they sat down to work his design in what she was later to describe as 'a simple rough way'. When it was finished they hung it on their bedroom wall, and Morris began to draw a set of panels for the dining room based on Chaucer's *Illustrious Women*. Later three of them were made into a screen which is now in the Morris Room at the Victoria and Albert Museum [68, 69, 71, 75, 76].

opposite
60 A runner designed and worked by May Morris.

overleaf
61 Design for an embroidered chair seat showing verdure and flowers, by May Morris.

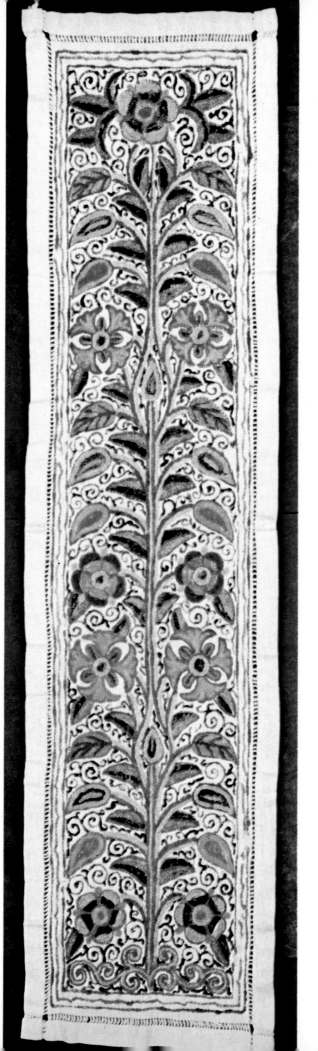

overleaf
62 *Hanging designed by William Morris. See also illustrations 63 and 64.*

opposite
63 *The well-turned corner, a detail of the hanging illustrated on the preceding page.*

64 *Detail showing the stitching and shading in the hanging in illustration 62.*

Clearly Morris was fascinated by the intracies of embroidery and by its subtle colours. Lecturing in 1888 on textile design he remarked that the aim of embroidery should be the exhibition of beautiful material. It was not worth doing, he suggested, unless it was very rich, very copious, or very delicate. 'For such an art,' he said, 'nothing patchy or scrappy or half-starved should be done; there is no excuse for doing anything which is not strikingly beautiful.' How keenly he was interested in stitches is well illustrated in a letter he wrote on 13 April 1876 to his friend Thomas Wardle of Leek, who co-operated with him in his efforts to revive the lost art of vegetable dyeing. He enclosed two examples of Cretan embroidery which, because the colours had faded through much washing, he was pleased with. But as well as this he had looked at the stitches and now commended them to the attention of Mrs Wardle, founder of the Leek Embroidery Society, as he was sure she would find them of considerable interest. Similarly, in a note to one of his embroiderers, Mrs Henry Holliday, wife of the noted designer of stained glass, he criticises a piece of work she had done for him on the grounds that it was rather too frail for the purpose for which it was intended, probably a cushion cover, suggesting that she should 'quilt down' some of the longer stitches with hair lines of silk *even at the expense of losing some of the beauty*. It may be an unusual use of the word 'quilting' but the meaning is plain. More important is the fact that Morris realised what every embroiderer knows to her cost: that a few long, straight, well-placed stitches will do something for a design that is entirely frustrated if, in the interest of commonsense, they are held down with even the most inconspicuous of couching stitches.

It was of course entirely due to the long hours Morris spent in Thomas Wardle's dye shop that the crewel wools we associate with art needlework were so soft and luminous and tender in colour. 'If you look at the pieces of colour that

65 Detail from a frieze depicting scenes from Chaucer's Romaunt of the Rose *designed by Edward Burne-Jones in collaboration with William Morris in 1872. It was worked by Margaret, wife of Sir Lothian Bell, and her daughter Florence for their home, Rounton Grange, the house designed by Philip Webb for Sir Lothian.*

delight you most,' he told the students at the Birmingham School of Art in 1894, 'as, for example, a Persian carpet or an illuminated book of the middle ages, and analyse its elements, you will be surprised at the simplicity of it, the few tints used, and the modesty of the tints, and therewithal all the clearness and precision of the outlines.' Reading May Morris's book on *Decorative Needlework* published in 1893 it is easy to see from whom she learnt to shade with crewel wools and silks. And the notes for her lessons show how good a teacher she was, and how sympathetic with the beginner's difficulties.

> In arranging your work [she wrote], you should have a definite scheme of colour, as simple as possible at first, and consisting of perhaps one predominating colour and a few touches of another for relief. When a little more experienced you should have some dominating colour among which contrasting shades are placed, bringing out the relative values according to your skill and instinct in choosing . . . When you feel you can come to bolder contrasts, avoid placing a blue directly against a green of nearly the same tone; if blue and green are mixed, the blue must be light against dark green, or the reverse. Again red and yellow, if both vivid, will need a softening line to separate them, though a pale yellow, and a pure, rather delicate scarlet is by no means a displeasing arrangement; or again a full, clear yellow and a very pale brick red . . . but avoid like poison the yellowish-brown green of a sickly hue that professes to be 'artistic' and looks like nothing but corruption.

It is, of course, the way in which a painter, not an embroiderer, expresses herself; and indeed her watercolour design for a chair seat [61] shows how able an artist May Morris might have become. Instead, with total self-abnegation, she identified herself completely with her father's work. No artist, in her eyes, came up to him. It did not make for a happy life. Proud, shy, and reserved she rarely allowed others to look into her heart. In a touching letter that she wrote to Emery Walker from 225 Riverside Drive, New York, on 21 February 1910, we are for a moment able to understand her.

> I *ought* to be bored, but I'm not. The glitter and the movement of the streets is amusing, the air is invigorating, the building is so absurd as to be fantastic, the types of faces one sees flit by are strangely varied, and I watch them like faces in a dream. The fact is I have thrown off the burden of work and anxiety for the moment and have done (I do believe) the almost impossible thing of getting outside my own skin, and putting on a temporary one. This is particularly refreshing for a person with my complaint of discontent, and I am thankful for the absurd enjoyment of the passing hour.

A year later, still living on her memories, she wrote again to Emery Walker.

> This time last year I was on the high seas. Do you know the stories of people who travel once to fairyland and can never find it again, and are restless ever afterwards? Fancy USA as fairyland!

66 Teaching crewel work—preparatory notes by May Morris for one of her classes.

How happily it seems she could have lived in her own present, and how much she might have contributed to the new direction embroidery was taking at the Glasgow School of Art under her great contemporaries, Jessie Newberry and Ann Macbeth. Instead we think of her writing up the impeccably kept day books in the embroidery workroom at Morris & Company, or else as a solitary figure in the tapestry room at Kelmscott, on the upper reaches of the Thames near Lechlade. It was the background into which Morris's romantic ideas about embroidery fitted perfectly.

In his story, the first of the greaty fantasy novels, *The Wood Beyond the World*, Morris seems to be thinking of embroidery as a kind of magic. He describes in limpid prose how Golden Walter travels into a dim and distant country and rescues the beautiful Maid from the power of a gnomish monster and his mistress. In their precipitate flight they stop to rest beside a spring, and Walter watches as the Maid gathers wild flowers, decks herself with garlands, and ties them into nosegays with which she decorates the simple, short sleeved white coat she is wearing, and is saddened because he thinks she does not know how quickly they will fade. But she can read his thoughts and bidding him watch, she touches each flower, and 'Lo, the meadow-sweet was crisp and clear again, the eye-bright blossoms shining, and the eglantine roses open once more.' When at last they reach the real world again the Maid loses her magical powers, but the posies do not fade. Instead they are embroidered.

67 May Morris in the tapestry room at Kelmscott, painted by M.H. Sloane.

A Royal School of Needlework

Ten years after Morris & Company opened its doors to the public, another important event in the history of crewel work took place. In 1873 the Royal School of Needlework or, as it was known at the time, the Royal School of Art-Needlework, was founded. It was not unique, being only one of a number of organisations dedicated to the encouragement of embroidery, whose charitable intention was to provide suitable employment for 'reduced and distressed gentlewomen'. With the exception of the Ladies' Work Society which celebrates its centenary in 1975, the Royal School has outlived them all.

The idea of founding a training school attached to a workroom and a showroom was first discussed by two friends in, we are told, the autumn of 1872. They were almost certainly Lady Welby and Mrs Anastasia Dolby, the author of a book on church needlework and the School's first director. Her death within a few months of the opening was a tremendous blow. It was as though the keystone had dropped out of the arch.

In 1886 the first chairman of the Council, Lady Mary Alford, published a book called *Needlework as Art*. The title tells us a great deal about the ideals of the founders whose principal aim, as spelt out in the prospectus, was 'to restore the beautiful and almost lost Art of embroidery to the high place it once held amongst the decorative arts'. Embroidery was neither a playful pastime nor, as many ladies seemed to think, was it synonymous with Berlin work. It was Art. William Morris had proved this. Like him the members of the Council were against the Industrial Revolution and the machine age.

68 One of a series of twelve figures based on Chaucer's Illustrious Women *that William Morris designed and helped to work for Red House. Other embroiderers included Jane Morris and her sister Elizabeth Burden, who later taught at the Royal School of Needlework. By 1865, when the family moved from Red House, seven panels were completed. Later three of them were made into a screen which is now in the Morris Room at the Victoria and Albert Museum. See illustrations 69 and 71 for details, and 75 for a second figure.*

Few persons [they wrote] are conscious how great a loss to the nation is involved in the universal substitution of machine printed and woven designs for hand-made decoration. The one advantage of the former has been their cheapness . . . In all other respects the superiority of hand-made ornamentation can hardly be disputed.

Morris having revived the art of embroidery with crewel wools, they set out to follow faithfully in his footsteps.

To be a lady *and* indigent was the yardstick for admission to the training school. Each applicant had to supply the names of two referees 'of undoubted reputation' to vouch for her, and the letter customarily sent to them read

Sir,

Miss . . . who is a candidate for admission to this School refers me to you to answer the following questions:
1   Is she a gentlewoman by birth and education?
2   Is she in need of remunerative employment?
3   Do you consider her in every way suited to our Association of Ladies?

Yours etc

But even for the most socially acceptable there were still two more hazards to be overcome. Before they were admitted to the workroom or entrusted with customers' material to take home, they had to attend a course of nine lessons, the fee for which was nine guineas. Not every experienced embroiderer wished to become a pupil, and not all could pay the fee, but both were obligatory and only in very exceptional cases was the fee waived. If, during the course, the teacher decided for some reason that the candidate was unsuitable, she informed her it was unlikely she would be able to make her work profitable. It was then up to the unhappy woman to decide whether to complete the course or to accept two-thirds of the fee and leave at once. Those responsible for drawing up these conditions comforted themselves with the reflection that this unfortunate state of affairs was unlikely to occur often as it was generally agreed that 'any lady of moderate intelligence' would have little difficulty in mastering the lessons; and with the best of intentions they added a special clause to the Rules that when two sisters or other near relations lived together, one might enter as a pupil and teach the other at home. Wisely they insisted that all workers should live in London, and made arrangements for those who had some distance to travel to take home extra work 'the doing of which would help to defray the expense of going backwards and forwards'. As in all ordinary commercial workrooms all work was the property of the School and was paid for by the piece. This sensible arrangement encouraged the quicker workers who could make considerably more than the 30 shillings a week earned by the average embroiderer.

69 Detail of the medieval turf bank which forms a continuous border along the bottom of the William Morris panels—this is a detail from the screen on the preceding page. Some silk and gold thread was used in these panels.

Every worker was held responsible for her mistakes. This of course depended on her receiving the correct instructions from the girls in the showroom, over which many problems seem to have arisen. In January 1878 the secretary penned this circular.

In consequence of the losses which the school has suffered from orders being incorrectly executed, it has been found necessary to make a rule that *each* person will be held responsible for errors occuring through her fault, either in the *taking of orders, spoiling of material, misdirecting parcels,* or naming a *price* verbally on her own opinion.

Ladies in the Show Room are particularly requested in all cases to enquire full addresses, and where foreign or difficult names are given to ask for the spelling. To be most careful that *the measurements are given by the customer* exactly, and not left to the judgment of the School as to allowance for hanging, etc.

That every particular is entered in the order book, as to price, time of execution, etc, and that no guesses should be given on their own responsibility. All letters and directions received in the Show Room to go direct to Miss Higgin.

Miss Higgin was herself an accomplished needlewoman who in 1880 compiled *A Handbook of Needlework* with the object of supplying useful hints to those unable to attend classes at the School, and to remind past students 'of the many little details which might easily be forgotten when their lessons are over'. It was edited by Lady Mary Alford and illustrated with designs available at the School including those by William Morris, Burne-Jones, and Gertrude Jekyll. It also contains an interesting section on 'Crewels and How to Use Them', and a few stitch diagrams, including one for feather stitch which she describes as being 'vulgarly called long and short stitch, long stitch, and sometimes embroidery stitch'.

Crewel [wrote Miss Higgin] should be cut in short threads, never more than half the length of a skein. If a long needleful is used, it is not only apt to pull the work, but is very wasteful, as the end is liable to become frayed or knotted before it is worked up. If it is necessary to use it double, care should be taken never to pass it through the eye of the needle knotting the two ends; but two separate threads of the length required should be passed together through the needle.

She also has this to say about the Bolton or Workhouse Sheeting, recommended as being the nearest available material to that used for crewel work in the seventeenth century: it is, she wrote,

a coarse twilled cotton fabric, seventy two inches wide, of a beautifully soft creamy colour, which improves much in washing, and an excellent ground for embroidery . . . It resembles the twilled cotton on which so much of the old crewel embroidery was worked in the seventeenth century, and is one of the most satisfactory materials when of really good quality.

Having established the training school and the workroom, the council next turned its attention to ladies who wished to be taught the fascinating new technique of art needlework. So began the non-vocational classes that are still a feature of the School's life. First, last, and all the time, the basic teaching was in crewel work, for what better training in surface stitchery could there be? In August 1880 the following instructions were issued for the guidance of those recruited from the staff to conduct these classes.

70 Embroidering the pall for Queen Victoria's funeral at the Royal School of Needlework. The original drawing by Anton Van Anrooy and W.L. Bruckman was reproduced in the Illustrated London News, *vol 118, 155, 1901.*

Each pupil will be provided with a small piece of Linen on which portions of various Designs illustrating the different stitches will be drawn. For these, and for the Crewels used during the Lessons, no charge will be made; but they will be retained by the Teacher—being the property of the School.

Samplers on Linen, containing various stitches, will be supplied if desired by the Pupil, with the crewels for working, at a charge of 4s od to 5s od according to the size and number of sprays on each. These are, of course, the Pupil's own property, and may be taken home between the Lessons for Practice and retained at the end of the Lessons.

The Teacher will also take with her some pieces of prepared and commenced work, such as Cushions, Chair-back Covers, or Footstools, so that pupils may, if they choose, purchase the work and take their lessons on it.

The fee for six lessons in crewel work was £1 4s od; £1 16s od for two members of the same family; and £2 8s od for three. Later there were to be courses in silk and ecclesiastical embroidery for which the fees were higher, but crewel work was obviously by far the most popular and was looked upon as a stepping stone to these dizzy heights. Children were encouraged to attend classes with their mothers, and in 1896 a special course for 'School-Room Girls' under sixteen was announced. It was held on Thursdays from 2 to 4 pm at a fee of 30 shillings. They were taught fine sewing, patching, darning, and buttonhole making. Needless to say, they also learnt crewel work.

As the School's reputation grew, requests were received for teachers to conduct classes in various parts of the country, and in October 1882 a course in art needlework was held at Cambridge. The teacher came down each week from London carrying a bag of embroideries worked at the School and returned with orders for prepared and finished work.

To its other activities the School now added the repair of old embroideries and tapestries, a service still performed in its workroom, and in 1881 it was ready to advance a step further. The following notice was duly circulated.

It having been represented to the Authorities of the Royal School of Art-Needlework that Architects find some difficulty in having their own designs carried out in Embroidery for Church Decoration, the Committee beg to announce that they are prepared to execute such Ecclesiastical Work from designs supplied to them by Architects or Artists, and that the colouring and detail of the Embroidery, when decided, will be submitted to the personal direction of the designer.

It would be difficult not to see the hand of William Morris at work here.

By 1884 the School was self-supporting. This was in no small measure due to the amount of crewel work produced in the workroom set aside for this particular method. A pair of curtains in crewels on serge or linen cost from £10 to

71 Detail of the hand, sword, and clothing of the figure in illustration 68.

£60; chair backs on linen from 14s 6d to £2 10s 0d; and folding screens from £13 to £100. There was also a ready market for prepared work and crewels for this could be purchased in the shop at 8d a one ounce skein. Ladies requiring larger quantities could buy it in quarter pound bundles of assorted shades which cost between 3s 0d and 4s 0d.

But the most famous project tackled by the crewel work studio was Walter Crane's *Complete Design for the Decoration of a Room with Hangings* which he devised for the Philadelphia Centennial Exhibition of 1876. It received the highest possible award, the School's reputation in America was made, and soon urgent requests were being received for a member of the staff to go and take charge of Philadelphia's own School of Art Needlework. The set included a frieze with figures of the arts on a green background; two portières with valances; a dado; a wall hanging on gold twill with figures representing the Four Elements; and several panels for covering pilasters. It was shown in Paris at the International Exhibition of 1878 and became the *pièce de résistance* of the School's first exhibitions.

To see the Royal School's exhibition became as much part of the London season as a visit to the Royal Academy, and it was not long before examples of historical embroideries were shown beside work done at the School itself. The draft of the letter sent to those likely to lend items from their collections still exists, and they responded with prompt generosity. There was virtually the whole of Lord Middleton's collection, now in the Castle Museum, Nottingham; the Clare Chasuble and the Syon Cope; the Chipping Campden Cope; and the vestments from Stoneyhurst College. In return the Royal School received more and more invitations to lend work to other exhibitions.

But success had its disadvantages, and with dismay the council heard that the School's exclusive designs were being copied by its commercial rivals. So another leaflet had to be printed, requesting the public to note that

> No designs on pricked paper, or in any other form than commenced work, are or ever have been sold by the School or supplied to any Agent. Further, no tracing powder is used in preparing the patterns sold for the purpose. All Designs, therefore, offered as those of the Royal School are either entirely spurious, or are pirated from their's.

It is interesting that at no time were any of either the School's designs or those of Morris & Company made into transfers.

On 23 June 1899 the School reached its zenith. From its modest beginnings over a bonnet shop in Sloane Street it had rapidly outgrown all its other premises and was now to have its own splendid building in the midst of the museums in South Kensington. The Prince of Wales laid the foundation stone, the Life Guards turned out, the choir of the Royal College of Music sang 'How pleasant is this sea-girt isle', the Bishop of London offered a prayer, and the proceedings closed with the singing of The Old Hundredth. It was largely due to the efforts of Morris & Company and the Royal School of Needlework that the ladies who attended this stirring ceremony went home to rooms furnished with hangings and cushions in crewel work. So great was the School's influence that in America the embroiderers had begun to call crewel work 'South Kensington embroidery'.

On 12 January 1906 a group of past students of the Royal School formed a society called The Society of Certificated Embroideresses of the Royal School of Needlework. At the next meeting held on 16 February it seemed to have dawned upon everybody that this was an unwieldy title, for it was changed to The Society of Certificated Embroideresses. It was agreed that membership should be open only to those holding the teacher's diploma and the two year certificate of the training school; that non-certificated students might join by invitation as associate members; and that the annual subscription should be 2s 6d. On 9 November the vexed question was argued as to whether the society should be affiliated to the Royal School. Eventually it was decided that this was not possible, and that non-teaching, non-professional embroiderers should be able to apply for membership, provided their work was of an acceptable standard.

Advice was now sought from Walter Crane, Lewis Day, and Sir Charles Holroyd, director of the National Gallery, on how the new society should be formed. Then came the First World War. In 1920, when meetings began again, it became the Embroiderers' Guild with Louisa Pesel as president, and before the year was out Mrs Lewis Day had become vice-president, Mrs Guy Antrobus, Mrs Newberry, and Miss Hogarth had joined the committee, and Mrs M. E. Rolleston had lectured to members on 'Embroidery on Costume of the Sixteenth and Seventeenth Centuries', a paper which she subsequently published in *The Embroideress*. In 1922 the Guild held its first exhibition and weekly classes in embroidery were conducted by Mrs Newall and Miss Hogarth.

Gradually its programme of classes, lectures, exhibitions, and visits was evolved. It began to build up its library, and from members' gifts emerged its notable collection of both historical and contemporary embroidery.

A Knight in Shining Armour

For convenience we divide art history into periods. We talk about the medieval, the Gothic, the baroque, the rococo, and the neo-classical periods, all of which have their effect upon the embroiderer's patterns. But they are purely artificial, a device to make communication about a difficult subject easier. It would be wrong, therefore, to suppose that they can be measured out between two dates with the same precision that the embroiderer counts her threads in pulled work or on canvas. Nor can they be fitted together neatly like patchwork with the untidy edges turned down all round and hidden from sight. They are more like the irregularly shaped and multi-coloured pieces of semi-transparent material from which the contemporary embroiderer creates her panels and hangings, applying one upon the other so that each in turn grows out of those already there, changes its appearance, and makes its own contribution to the whole, anticipating, at the same time, the shape and colour of those that come after it. So although the Victorian period ended officially with the death of the Queen, the seeds of the future had already been sown and come into flower; while at the same time the Morris tradition still lived on, for taste, like period styles, cannot be arbitrarily and instantaneously changed. There is no moment at which all embroiderers enjoy working the same type of pattern; only constantly overlapping styles and tastes. There will always be some who prefer the well-tried and familiar to the new and adventurous.

So when in 1909 Lady Mary Trevelyan of Cambo in Northumberland decided to embark upon a panel in crewel work for the house at Wallington, where she would eventually live and where Lady Julia Calverley's canvas work panels were already hanging [39], it was only natural that she should want it designed in the still popular though declining Morris style. She commissioned a young man of nineteen, John Edgar Pratt, who subsequently became principal of the Edinburgh School of Art, to make the sketch and draw up the cartoon. Then on 6 July 1910 she put in the first stitch. Her frame stood in a corner window of the house in Cambo village where she and her husband lived and brought up their family. She liked to work for an hour each morning before breakfast, and when Parliament was in session and the family moved to London, the panel was rolled up and taken with them.

72 *Watercolour sketch of Lady Trevelyan working her panel, by P. Bicknell, 1925.*

The panel [73] is worked throughout in long and short stitch with French crewel wools. Cut off from her supplies during the First World War, Lady Trevelyan had to fall back on English wools, and found them sadly disappointing. She marked the place on which she was working at the time and where the colours have faded badly with the words 'May 1917 at War'. The design was drawn on three pieces of linen and when the embroidery was finished Lady Trevelyan herself sewed them together, embroidering over the joins so cleverly that it is almost impossible to discover where they are. Unlike the borders on the Bayeux Tapestry, these were worked separately and added as a final touch.

For anyone with a family tradition going back to a legendry ancestor who fought under King Arthur's banner and sat at his Round Table, and who not only admired the work of William Morris but was also in sympathy with his liberal educational and political views, Lady Trevelyan naturally had little difficulty in choosing a subject for her panel. It had to be a knight in shining armour. The pennant with the motto *Tyme Tryeth Troth*, and the coats-of-arms of her own and her husband's families, all found convenient places for themselves, and in the best Morris tradition there is a legend worked in bright yellow silk, outlined in a couched gold thread, that reads: *From St Michael's Mount the Knights of King Arthur's court strove for a wager to swim ashore. Sir Trevelyan alone wins to land.* Behind it is an old Cornish story that recounts how, after Arthur's death, the knights were challenged to swim their horses to the mainland. One by one they sank beneath the waves, only the mighty Sir Trevelyan reaching the shore in safety. It is interesting to find that Lady Trevelyan did not care for the figures of the drowning knights that Pratt included in the original sketch, and left them out.

Before it was set up at Wallington, Lady Trevelyan lent the panel to a number of exhibitions and it was also shown in London. Knowing that every embroiderer who saw it would be interested in its hidden symbolism, she wrote a few brief notes on it and also on the dates at which various parts were worked. It must be one of the best documented examples of crewel work in existence. For once we are there beside the embroiderer as she works, looking over her shoulder and watching the design grow. We see her completing the upper border during the first week of the First World War, and recording the armistice on the Trevelyan shield with a thin gold line on one of the waves from which the horse is rising. 'The Peace Treaty', she wrote, 'has its mark on the red collar of the big horse; it is in white, but would have been in gold had the Treaty been more satisfactory.' Then there were the intimate, family events to be added. In 1913 she recorded the birth of her fourth child, Marjorie Trevelyan, by working her initials on the back of the Knight's helmet; and when in 1920 her son Geoffrey was born, she worked his initials on the front fold of the saddle cloth. One of the small fish in the lower border records the birth of her first grandchild, Susan Dower.

In 1924, when Ramsay MacDonald became head of the first Labour government, he invited Sir Charles Trevelyan to join his cabinet and appointed him President of the Board of Education. Lady Trevelyan celebrated the event by

73 Panel designed in 1909 by John E. Pratt and worked by Lady Mary Trevelyan between 1910 and 1933.

adding the date and the Prime Minister's initials to the top of the red scroll round the chestnut tree; and when in 1931 Sir Charles resigned, she added a band of his green and white election colours to the tip of the scroll that bears her own name, and nailed a little red flag to the masthead of the boat that appears in the lee of St Michael's Mount. The knight's plume she copied from a seagull's wing, and before working the great billowing cloud behind his head, studied the clouds in one of Titian's paintings in the National Gallery. And how encouraging to know that she had trouble with the Knight's face, the model for which was originally her husband. She was never satisfied with it. Out it came. In the end she asked her father's sister, a skilled and experienced embroiderer named Florence Johnson, to do it for her. She worked it on a fresh piece of linen on a small frame, and then applied it over the rejected one. It was only to be expected that the result would not be a happy one. Better by far for her to have left well alone. But every embroiderer is a perfectionist, perpetually dissatisfied with her own efforts, and sure that other embroiderers' work is so much better than her own.

Entr'acte IV

As an English embroideress, the spirit
moves me to take up my pen and protest
that I entirely disagree with all this!

Letter to the Editor of
The Embroideress, *1924*

What a strangely unpredictable subject embroidery is, perpetually shot through
with spasms of enlightenment, moments of invention, and protracted periods of
stagnation. Always the past and the present, the old-fashioned and the modern
exist side by side. More often than not they are at odds with each other. But
inevitably change must come. One day somebody catches sight of a new idea.
She mentions it to another embroiderer and finds that the same thought has
occurred to her. Other embroiderers living perhaps in different parts of the
country have the same experience. They have all seen something—a chair with
a new line, a textile with a new pattern, a plate with a new design—perhaps a
sentence in a book they are reading that has on the instant helped them to put
words around the thought they have been unconsciously aware of but have not
succeeded in articulating. Immediately they know where they are going and how
to get there. Confidently they hasten towards the future. Their patterns change
and they find new ways of working them. The new style they have introduced
climbs to its peak. It is taken up by other embroiderers. Then the manufacturers
of embroidery materials and the publishers of needlework magazines simplify
and popularise it. If they are lucky it will reach the dimensions of a craze. This
time they are really in the money. It happened to crewel work in this present
century. No self-respecting, progressively minded embroiderer would look at it.
It became the symbol of all she disliked most in embroidery; the dead hand of
the past laid upon the present frustrating her efforts to be contemporary.

A new line of thought

In 1864 Mrs William Rowat, wife of a Paisley shawl manufacturer, gave birth to a daughter. Like Dr John Gregory, Mr Rowat lost his wife, and like Mrs Knowles he believed in equal opportunities for women; so he sent his daughter to boarding school in Edinburgh and when she was eighteen, to spend a year in Italy. There she became fascinated by the early Italian painters, the mosaics at Ravenna, and peasant embroidery. On her return she decided to attend a session at the Glasgow School of Art, but before the year was out had embarked upon the full time course and was beginning to study design, textiles, and stained glass. In 1889 she married the principal, Francis H. Newberry, and in 1894 started a class for embroidery in the art school.

At first Jessie Newberry taught in the tradition of William Morris, using crewel wools in long and short stitch on linen, but soon she started to develop her own highly personal style, working not only in crewel but also in applied linen, and devising patterns in which she contrasted long meandering stems with straight lines, and flowers with lettering. An enthusiastic and knowledgeable gardener, it is believed that the flat round roses she created from circles of linen cut out freehand and applied with an outline of satin stitch, were the prototype of the famous 'Glasgow Rose' motif characteristic of the work of the Glasgow school of designers [81].

In 1910, when illness compelled Jessie Newberry to give up teaching, one of her ex-students, Ann Macbeth, took over from her. In due course she in turn trained Mary Swanson as her assistant.

Ann Macbeth inherited her artistic talents from her grandfather, Norman Macbeth, a member of the Royal Scottish Academy. She too took the full art course at the Glasgow School of Art, but was soon drawn to Jessie Newberry's embroidery classes. An energetic and prolific worker, she executed many large scale commissions and exhibited regularly with the Lady Artists' Club, as well as

74 Crewel work panel published by Mrs Rolleston in The Embroideress, *as an example of 'the true Jacobean spirit' brought up to date.*

in London, Edinburgh, and other centres. A fine draughtsman, she would often draw designs for others to work—anything rather than let them use transfers—but basically she tried to persuade them to make their own designs. To her regular art school teaching she added Saturday classes to which teachers in elementary schools flocked. Realising that they were ready and eager to introduce more liberal methods of teaching needlework, she and Mary Swanson published *Educational Needlework* in 1913. In it they proposed a revolutionary scheme for encouraging the child from the beginning to develop a sense of design and colour by decorating simple and useful objects with stitchery. So the sampler ceased to be an improving exercise and became a mat. Folded in half, with a draw-string threaded through the top, it became a bag. It could equally well become a pocket or an apron. Embroidery had become 'creative'.

By 1922 the interest in creative embroidery had become so widespread among teachers and students that the invaluable Mrs Rolleston published a series of reports in *The Embroideress* on the courses held in provincial art schools. In Volume 1 she printed an article by Isabel Catterson-Smith, daughter of the director of the Birmingham Municipal School of Art, where students approached embroidery with 'a happy playfulness' and from this initial freedom went on to make more restrained but highly imaginative designs. Next came a report by Kathleen Harris on the Manchester College of Art, and this was followed by one on the Edinburgh School of Art, where students' perception of line, form, and colour was sharpened by studying historical embroideries and by attending classes in plant form and design. At the College of Art in Bradford, embroidery was taught in relation to dress, but at Armstrong College, Newcastle, it was part of the regular curriculum of the Applied Art department and could be chosen as a subject in a four year diploma course. Like most other colleges, Sheffield encouraged its students to experiment with stitches and stressed the importance of embroidery designs embodying 'symbols or patterns of things that belong to our own time rather than to those that belong to a previous age'. At Leeds College of Art the writer described the students' excitement at finding how freely 'oddly assorted materials could be brought into happy relation with each other without troubling about scale, perspective or probability'. Mrs Rolleston illustrated this article with a panel worked in crewel wools in a way that she described as 'frankly and undeniably contemporary' [74].

At the same time, embroidery was being taught in London at the Royal College of Art by Mrs A. H. Christie; May Morris was a member of the Advisory Council of the Hammersmith College of Arts and Crafts; at the Central School of Arts and Crafts the principal declared that he was happy to encourage not only full-time but also part-time embroidery students; while at the Battersea College of Arts and Crafts embroidery students studied architecture, painting, sculpture, and the decorative arts. Virtually all this teaching was channelled into the needlework classes in elementary schools where it was fostered and encouraged along with so-called Child Art, by such progressive men as R.R.Tomlinson, who

75 A second figure from the series based on Chaucer's Illustrious Women *designed by William Morris for Red House. See following page for detail, and 68 for another figure.*

in 1935 came out strongly against the teacher who insisted on her pupils working antiquated samplers. In his *Crafts for Children* he presented embroidery as a natural outcome of the art class and pointed out that

> the teaching of stitches should be directed towards the making of simple repeating patterns, and to form a decorative scheme, or to decorate something, rather than the producing of a specimen or sampler.

Jessie Newberry, Ann Macbeth, and Mary Swanson had done their work well.

In 1933, when Lady Trevelyan finished her Knight in Shining Armour, the *avant-garde* embroiderer had begun to look with disapproval at art needlework. According to many writers, embroidery was either colourful, spontaneous, and *unconscious*, like peasant embroidery; or else it was, like art needlework, contrived, artificial, and *conscious*. No praise was too high for the former, no censure too sharp for the latter. Crewel work had become the whipping boy of the progressive embroiderer, and the craze of everybody else. The more vigorously it was promoted by the needlework magazines and the manufacturers of embroidery materials and transfers, the more she despised it. All the same, there was hardly an English middle class home without its Queen Anne style cushions, its Jacobean curtains and pelmets, its Stuart firescreen, and its Period Embroidery coffee table cloth, or a housewife without her work bag embroidered on a Penelope fabric in Penelope crewel wools.

The alert Mrs Rolleston fanned the flames with the pages of *The Embroideress*. In an article on 'The Influence of Jacobean Embroidery on Modern Work' she wrote in the fifty-fifth issue

> Not very many years ago a quite deliberate rebellion was started among modern needlewomen against the continuous and inexplicable cult of what is popularly known as 'Jacobean Embroidery'. It was felt by those thinkers that the slavish contentment with which people living over 200 hundred years later, under entirely different conditions, copied, re-copied, and adapted with diminishing vitality, the splendid works of the second half of the seventeenth century must be put to an end somehow, even if, in the process of arousing the dreamers, many hard words would be exchanged and misunderstandings arise.

She went on, however, to imply that try as they might it was impossible to quench the essential vigour and energy of good crewel work. It had simply, she said, evaded its destroyers and assumed a more sophisticated form; proving her point by illustrating the article with a set of pictures in which she contrasted Abigail Pett's bed hangings [43] and the reverse side of the work bag [25], with examples of contemporary crewel work. From this she concluded that the new designs were strongly rooted in the past and warned that the present should never wholly throw off the fundamentally good qualities of the old in favour of more advanced

76 Detail of the face of the figure on the preceding page.

ideas. Over thirty years before Lewis F. Day had said exactly the same thing when he remarked that it is at least as foolish for the embroiderer to try to cut herself off from the past as to tether herself too tightly to it.

In 1929 Mrs Rolleston had obviously been pressed by her readers to explain exactly what was meant by 'modern' embroidery. She chose as a suitable example a picture designed by the painter Wyndham Tryon and worked by Mary Hogarth. With her pen dipped in acid she observed that 'Miss Hogarth has been able to prove that it is possible to carry out successfully in embroidery, a pattern originated by a painter'; adding sourly that this was not so great a wonder as her readers might suppose, it being 'no different from the accepted practice of medieval embroiderers'. The horsemen on the Bayeux Tapestry were surely being recalled from Valhalla to demolish the contemporary embroiderer!

But Mary Hogarth was not the person to be deterred by an unfavourable notice in an embroidery magazine. She was a rebel against anything that smacked of outmoded conventions and was heart and soul behind those who looked ahead rather than behind them. A painter of distinction, she admired the Art Nouveau designs of the Omega Workshops, and the teaching of Roger Fry, and was a personal friend of Sickert and Duncan Grant, who was currently drawing designs for Vanessa Bell to embroider. One of these pieces was included in an exhibition of contemporary embroidery organised at the Victoria and Albert Museum by the British Institute of Industrial Art in July 1933. Out of this came one of the *Studio* magazine's Special Publications entitled *Modern Embroidery*. It was edited by Mary Hogarth. Grasping the nettle firmly with both hands she declared in the foreword that

> Modern embroidery should be the invention of today in design and should express this age. The technique should be governed by the design.

Among the embroideries with which she illustrated the book was a picture executed in crewel wools by Aileen M. Booker [84]. The subject, a domestic interior, although not uncommon for a painting, was quite new in embroidery design. So was the thought behind it. It was not a needle painting. The embroiderer, we are told, began by making a quick watercolour sketch of the scene which she later organised into a more formal composition. To this, she added the cat. Probably doing no more than edit Aileen Booker's own words, Mary Hogarth wrote

> There is no intention to make the embroidery look like a painting, any more than one would want to make a painting look like embroidery, as the designer rightly considers they are two completely different mediums and should be treated as such.

For Mary Hogarth who, like May Morris, could not help expressing herself in terms of painting, the embroiderer was an artist, a designer in her own right, not an imitator. It was the thought behind her design that was important, and the way in which she realised it in mass, line, and colour. The stitches were her uniquely significant method of interpreting the design she herself had composed.

77 Wool picture worked by Miss Letitia Neill, c. 1910, from an original design.

A St Swithun's Day Enterprise

Winchester has many claims to fame. It was the capital city of two of England's most easily remembered kings—Alfred the Great and William the Conqueror. Its cathedral is celebrated as the see of a medieval bishop whose relics, since 971, have lain behind the high altar, and whose name is associated with one of the most popular and depressing pieces of English folklore: the legend that if it rains on 15 July, the Feast of St Swithun, it will continue to do so for forty days.

When William the Conqueror, fresh from the Battle of Hastings, arrived in Winchester he found St Swithun's old cathedral was being pulled down and rebuilt in the new Norman style. Of this building only the transepts remain. From the stone paved floor, buckled and bent with age, the rounded arches rise inexorably upwards in three tiers, like acrobats standing on each other's shoulders. In the south transept, in an open space that once formed part of the triforium gallery, are a number of documents that tell the story of a comparatively recent episode in the long history of the cathedral—the furnishing of the choir with cushions, kneelers, and alms bags. The person responsible for organising and directing the scheme was a distinguished embroiderer and teacher named Louisa Pesel, who lived not far from the cathedral in Colebrook Street. The letter in which she accepted the commission from the Dean and Chapter was written on 24 April 1931.

> I shall be very pleased to undertake the work you propose and feel honoured that you are willing to trust it to me . . .
>
> £25 will go a good way in wools and canvas though it will, I imagine, not cover it all. Shall we start with that and report when we are running out? I can get the wools wholesale, so that will be a decided help.

In this delightfully informal way a project that occupied some two hundred embroiderers for five years began. Louisa Pesel called it 'A St Swithun's Day Enterprise', and the embroiderers 'The Winchester Cathedral Broderers'. She herself was known as 'The Mistress of the Cathedral Broderers'.

Louisa Pesel was no newcomer to embroidery. As long ago as 1899 she had assisted W. G. Paulson Townsend with his book *Embroidery or the Craft of the Needle*, and from 1903 until 1907 had been in charge of the Royal Hellenic Schools for Embroidery and Laces in Athens. In 1925 the first of her *Leaves from my Embroidery Note Book* had been welcomed by the editor of *The Embroideress* who wrote

> We have no doubt that these sheets will be of the greatest benefit to those who are working on traditional lines, and who, in an age when good transfer patterns are almost unobtainable, welcome any opportunity of copying designs from one of the best periods of English embroidery. Miss Pesel's *Leaves* give plenty of scope, too, to the more ambitious worker who enjoys the problem of adapting and arranging her own patterns.

In the previous year the editor had published an article by Louisa Pesel herself in which she had set out to analyse the relationship between colour and stitchery. She came to the conclusion that if the embroidery was multi-coloured, the stitches, as in eastern embroideries, should be few and simple; but that if the embroiderer chose to use a variety of different stitches, they would show to greater advantage if she worked them in a limited range of colours or even in monochrome. She pointed out that on the English embroiderer's love of stitches and her ability to work in a severely restricted colour range, or in one colour only, depended the success not only of Elizabethan black work and eighteenth century white work, but also that of the early crewel work hangings. Of the latter she wrote

78 Sybil Blunt's watercolour sketch and notes from which the medallion in illustration 87 was worked.

Seen at close hand, the necessary interest is secured by the patterns on the big surfaces, being produced by changes in the density of the stitches, and they are light or heavy, open or closed, as the design demands.

As her notebook shows, Louisa Pesel was by no means an original designer. Her taste was for embroidery on the counted thread, and the patterns on many of the Winchester embroideries consist basically of roundels, interlacing bands, knots, and floral motifs that are mainly adaptations of seventeenth century samplers, particularly those in the Victoria and Albert Museum. Her strength lay in her technical expertise, her knowledge of stitches, and in her sense of colour. It was her friend Sybil Blunt, a watercolourist of no small skill, who provided the historical designs that were an integral part of the scheme.

Wherever she went Louisa Pesel studied historical embroideries, collected stitches, and made a garden. Her reputation as a collector and grower of irises stood as high as her reputation as an embroiderer. The deep soft blues and clear bright yellows she chose as the predominating colours of the crewel wools in which the kneelers and cushions were worked might have come straight out of her garden.

The intimate connection that exists between embroidery and gardening has seldom been fully appreciated by either embroiderers or gardeners. Louisa Pesel was perhaps an exception. So also was her contemporary, the celebrated

79 One of the original patterns devised by Sybil Blunt and Louisa Pesel for the long cushions in Winchester Cathedral.

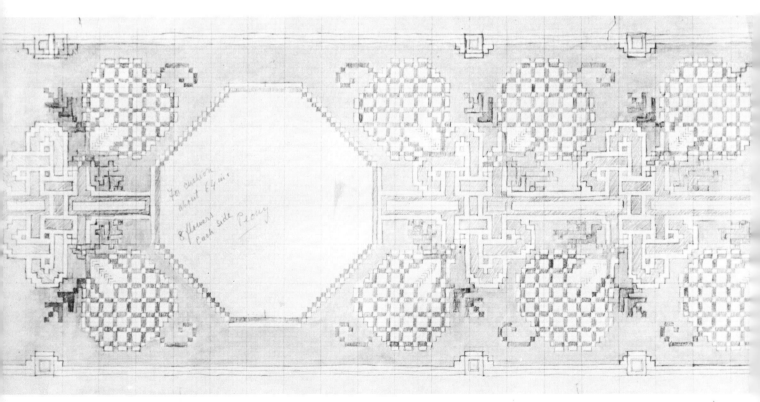

garden designer, Gertrude Jekyll, but then she too was an embroiderer although most people have forgotten that as a young woman she drew designs for the Royal School of Needlework, two of which were published by L. Higgin in her *Handbook of Needlework*. In her book *Colour Schemes for Gardens* she wrote

> I am strongly of the opinion that the possession of a quantity of plants, however good the plants may be, and however ample the number, does not make a good garden. Having got the plants, the great thing is to use them with careful selection and definite intention. It is just in the way it is done that lies the whole difference between commonplace gardening and gardening that may lightly be called a work of art.

If for 'plants' and 'gardening' we read 'stitches' and 'embroidery' we arrive at a statement uncannily like Louisa Pesel's ideas about embroidery.

80 Detail from the long cushion in illustration 87.

The area in the cathedral that was to be furnished with cushions and kneelers is bounded on two sides by a stone screen, joined at one end by the reredos behind the high altar, a nineteenth century confection of white sugary arcades and saintly figures, each burdened with an appropriate badge or symbol, and at the other by an elaborately carved wooden screen of amazing complexity and Gothic detail. This in turn joins the two sets of choir stalls and benches where the clergy and choir sit. Between them and the chancel steps is the bishop's throne, the pulpit, and a double set of chairs for the congregation. So Louisa Pesel had not one, but four tasks: to make kneelers for the chairs, cushions for the stalls, long cushions for the benches, and the alms bags.

The alms bags seem to have posed few problems and by 19 May 1932, when the Broderers in a special service, which until 1938 became a regular feature of the cathedral calendar, presented their year's work, ten had been completed. With them were offered 117 blue kneelers, one stall cushion, and literally yards of yellow borders from which the sides of the bench cushions would eventually be made. All this, as Louisa Pesel observed in her report, gave her and Sybil Blunt an opportunity to pick out the really good and artistic craftswomen to whom the task of interpreting the historical designs could be safely entrusted, and also to discover which colours and stitches would make the strongest impact in a building that seemed to lap up colour like a sponge.

Obviously it was on the cushions that they concentrated most of their time and energy. They were pleased when people remarked upon the colours they had chosen, likening them to bits of stained glass brought down from the windows to lighten the darker corners of the choir stalls. They were, in fact, not taken from the windows but from the small heraldic shields with which the two stone screens were studded. 'Bright mid-blue, a mid-red, and a rather light verdigris green and gilding' is how Louisa Pesel described them. And what an eye for colour she had!

> Blues have been used [she wrote] for the centre knots, a small quantity of green for the narrow leaves, and then endless shades of yellow to give a broken background which, because of the nature of the stitch, has almost the effect of *patina*.

The idea that by combining the right stitches and colours the embroiderer can introduce interesting textures, that is *patina*, into her work is now well known; and texture has become one of the measurable qualities by which the embroiderer's work is judged. Although for years teachers had encouraged their students to build up patterns from stitches, the idea of textures was still something of a novelty. How many hours and how many shades of yellow crewel wool Louisa Pesel used up in her efforts to develop this technique, history does

opposite
81 Cushion cover designed by Jessie Newberry and worked by Edith Rowat in 1899.

overleaf
82 Late nineteenth century embroidery in crewel wools, highlighted with silks, by Phoebe Traquair.

MY AUNT'S DRAWINGROOM   A.M. BOOKER

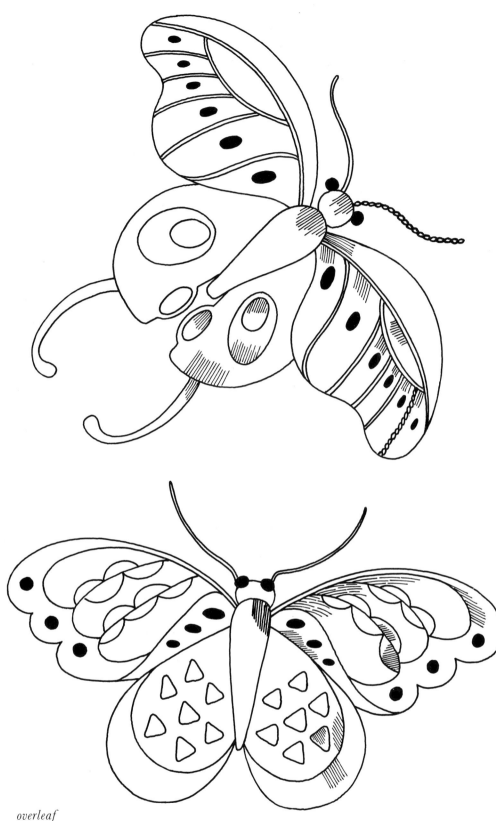

overleaf
83 Detail of Phoebe Traquair's panel.

opposite
84 My Aunt's Drawing Room *by Aileen Booker.*

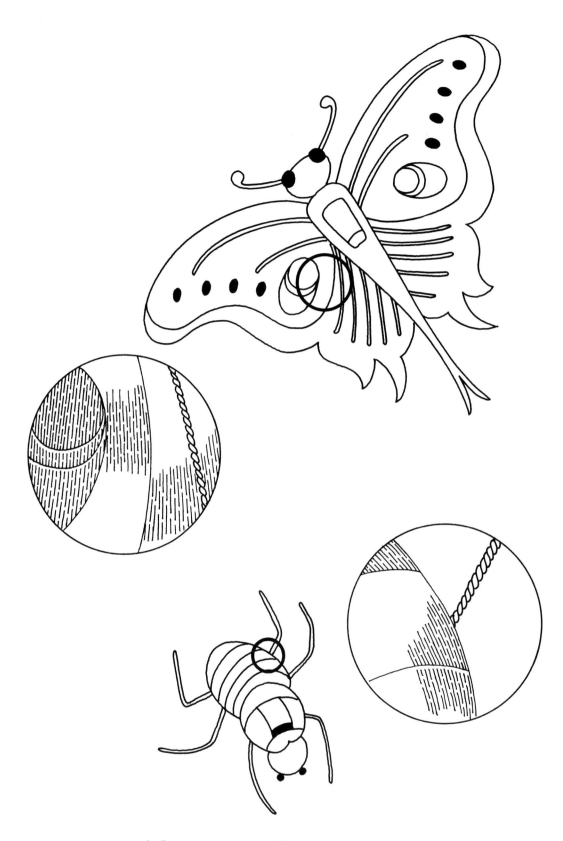

not record. Lesser women would have worked the background in cross stitch and left it at that. Louisa Pesel set about finding a combination of stitches and tones that each embroiderer could use in her own way, but without disturbing the harmony of the whole.

Eventually it was the Friends of the Cathedral who paid for the materials. They also provided the Broderers with rooms in which classes could be held, materials stored, records kept, designs copied, and work prepared for distribution. Perhaps more than anyone else Kathleen Little, who was one of the earliest Broderers and for much of the time supervised the preparation of the work, helped to maintain and extend the tradition that Louisa Pesel began. For twenty years she served on the Council of the Friends, retiring as recently as 1971. During all this time she cared for the cathedral needlework and vestments, and passed on her knowledge of kneeler making to countless other embroiderers. She died in January 1974.

Sybil Blunt spent three days a week at the rooms. In all she designed fifty-six medallions for the long cushions as well as those for the stall cushions. In 1934 a tiny booklet on the medallions was published for which she wrote the notes. Better even than this, from the embroiderer's point of view, is the fact that her sketches and designs have survived and now form part of the archive in the south transept. To be able to put them together with the notes and the completed embroideries is a unique experience for anybody with a sense of history, an eye for design and colour, and an interest in embroidery.

Sybil Blunt's designs are neither pretentious nor dramatic. The moments of decision and indecision are there for all to see. It is often obvious that the embroideries themselves are stronger and better than the sketches from which they were worked. But had they not been so faithfully researched, or drawn and painted with less casual charm, the Broderers could not have rendered them half so well. Here is a designer who did not set out to dominate: she provided a design and left its interpretation to others, secure in the knowledge that anybody who had been trained under Louisa Pesel's eye would know how to handle them. There is nothing commonplace about the result. In fact, as Gertrude Jekyll put it, the medallions may 'lightly be called a work of art'.

The final presentation of embroideries took place in the cathedral in July 1938. How many pounds of specially dyed crewel wool had been used up it is impossible to guess. There were

360 kneelers
96 alms bags
34 long cushions for benches
62 stall cushions
2 bench cushions for the choristers each 6 feet long, and
18 yards of side pieces for the communion rails

as well as a carpet for the lectern, furnishings for the bishop's throne and the lay clerks' seats, a special kneeler for the litany desk, and the sides for twenty-four chapter kneelers. The pattern on which all future kneeler schemes would be based had been established.

On one of the medallions Sybil Blunt depicted the coming of the Normans to commemorate the arrival of William the Conqueror in Winchester. It brings the story of the use of crewel wools by English embroiderers full circle, for on it she drew some of the French ships from the Bayeux Tapestry [78, 87].

A family affair

When Louisa Pesel told the Dean of Winchester that she knew of a firm from which she could obtain the hard wearing canvas and fast dyed crewel wools she needed for her St Swithun's Day Enterprise, she had in mind the small family firm of Arthur H. Lee & Sons of Birkenhead in Cheshire.

In 1888 Arthur Lee, who throughout his life sought to make his firm's products better rather than cheaper, set out to create a new line in furnishing fabrics in part of a weaving shed in Warrington. Twenty years later, when his sons joined him, they built a new factory at Birkenhead. In succeeding years it was to be extended many times.

At first the firm's patterns were drawn by Arthur Lee's brother-in-law, an architect named G. F. Armitage, but before long he was also commissioning them from such prominent designers as Walter Crane and Charles Voysey. However when he began inventing new techniques, it was only natural that he should find the most successful patterns were those he drew himself. So unlike William Morris, who learnt to weave in order to be able to design furnishing fabrics, Arthur Lee's designs developed out of his knowledge of the loom itself. He was particularly interested in improving the Jacquard loom, invented by a Frenchman of that name at the beginning of the nineteenth century, by means of which the appearance of embroidery could be successfully imitated. In this it differed from the embroidering machine, invented by another Frenchman named Joshué Heilmann in 1828, that actually reproduced the stitches of embroidery.

In spite of the new weaves made possible by the Jacquard loom, Lee chaffed at the limited range of colours he could use. He was utterly frustrated by the fact that with the power loom he had not the same freedom to employ as many colours as the hand weaver, the tapestry weaver, or the embroiderer. So he hit upon the idea of over-printing a patterned textile with coloured wood blocks, entrusting its development to his son Christopher Lee, who was eventually to succeed him as president of the company. The result was a furnishing fabric marketed as Jacquard-woven Hand-blocked Tapestry. The process was an exacting one. In order to fit the woven pattern each block was usually no more than three inches across, and a great many might be required to over-print a single pattern. The problem was to find and train girls with a natural aptitude for the work. They had to be ambidexterous, have a good memory for shapes, and, as Christopher Lee himself put it, be able to think of at least five things at once, not only for a few minutes, but all the time. From adding block printed colours to a woven pattern it was only a step to embroidering it.

In a paper read to the Royal Society of Arts on 16 November 1966, Christopher Lee explained how, shortly before the First World War, his father had been asked by an American furniture manufacturer whether he could reproduce a piece of old embroidery on his Jacquard loom. It was just the sort of challenge calculated to appeal to Arthur Lee, and led directly to his taking an embroidered pattern from an Elizabethan long cushion in the Victoria and Albert Museum, and reproducing the hunting scene on it by the hand-blocking technique. Marketed as *The Horseman* it was to prove one of the firm's most popular designs. It prompted Christopher Lee to say

> A design is like a book or a play in that no one, including the critics, knows whether or not the public will like it or reject it, until it is displayed in the shops, or read, or the curtain goes up in the theatre.

The firm's interest in embroidery took another direction when, sometime in 1910, one of the brothers returned from London with a piece of canvas work in tent stitch. This led to the manufacture of an entirely new textile which appeared at first sight to be covered all over with long thin rows of flawless tent stitch. It was called Pin Weave or 300 Cloth. Lee taught his embroiderers to work repeating patterns in crewel wools on it, forming their tent stitches over those already mechanically produced on it. By eliminating the slow, tedious process of covering the background with stitches, canvas work on a large scale had become a commercial proposition. Realising not only the length of time it took to make hand woven tapestries but also their prohibitive cost, the versatile Lees set about making panels and hangings worked in tent stitch on their 300 Cloth. Their design and manufacture became the special responsibility of Christopher Lee's son Stephen. By using a variety of stitches he made his 'Needle-work Tapestries' look, from a distance, like genuine canvas work. One of the largest commissions he undertook was a set of hangings for the board room in the head office of the Midland Bank in London. It involved the working of over fifteen and a half million stitches.

Inevitably crewel work made its appearance in the workroom. It was marketed as 'Crewel Craft Hand Embroidery'. The patterns were largely traditional and were worked on a very heavy all-wool upholstery cloth in long and short stitch, with anything up to four threads in the needle at once. Each flower and leaf is as hard and tightly packed with stitches as human hands can make it, and there is just as much wool on the wrong side of the work as on the right.

Like William Morris, Arthur Lee based his original colour range on vegetable dyes, but gradually as new and improved dye stuffs became available, he found he could use them more easily and with equally good effect, and soon his embroiderers had 240 shades of crewel wool at their disposal. No wonder that Louisa Pesel with her sensitive eye for colour should have had the crewels for her Cathedral Broderers dyed by Arthur H. Lee & Sons. In due course they also wove for her the famous 'Winchester Canvas' from which the kneelers and cushions were made. The wools, the dyes, and the canvas have stood the test of forty years constant wear and exposure to light.

When a few years ago the firm went out of business and the stock was sold, many embroiderers took advantage of the opportunity to acquire fabrics and crewels of a standard they knew they were unlikely to see again. One of them, a teacher named Mary Hancock, reluctant to see their 'Crewel Craft' disappear, bought up a few of their old travellers' samples and set to work to find out how it had been done. Then, using Appleton's crewel wools, she began to adapt the technique. She evolved a slightly different style, rendering the pattern in even higher relief, and passed it on to a class of mature students. In effect she had put an ingenious commercial variant of traditional crewel work back into the hands of the embroiderer—and there are many of them—who is herself a traditionalist, a craftsman rather than an artist, who is delighted by both subtle colours and the freedom of surface stitchery, but who would never be happy with a pattern she herself had drawn [88].

85 The Pagoda Tapestry, *a chinoiserie design for a furnishing fabric by Arthur H. Lee & Sons.*

Epilogue

One figure coloured slightly over is not
rightly discerned until it be finished so
this book is not discerned till the end be
viewed; it is a Miscellany and not otherwise
to be respected, not learned, and therefore
the easier to be pardoned.

All I hope that see it are my Friends and
accept it friendly. So willing your friendly
favour, I leave it to your viewing.

Thomas Trevelyon, 1608

From time to time there come to every embroiderer moments of the purest possible pleasure. The particular piece of work on which she has been engaged is finished. She removes it from the frame and spreads it out between her hands, examining every detail with minute attention. It is as though she is seeing it for the first time. Out of her own skill, initiative, and invention she has created something that pleases her. Briefly she allows herself to savour her sense of satisfaction and fulfilment.

Maybe, she concedes, it is not of quite such surpassing excellence as she had hoped to achieve when she made the design, chose the threads, and decided exactly where to place the first stitch, but on balance as good as or even a little better than her previous work.

Will anybody else, she wonders, realise how much thought and care has gone into it? Will it by some happy chance be miraculously preserved, forgotten but not destroyed, eventually to become a treasured family heirloom, and even perhaps to find its way into a great museum, where scholars will document it and embroiderers study it as an interesting example of 'historical' needlework? Surely, she reflects, it is not asking very much to be remembered as a woman who was clever with her needle.

86 *In 1974 Joyce Judd, a mature student attending a weekly class at the Royal School of Needlework, devised this motif from traditional sources. It is mounted on a 12 inch square frame and is worked on white vyella, backed with linen, in Appleton's rose red crewel wools range 940, numbers 3, 5, 6, 7, 8, plus a little white. The thirty-one stitches include feather, chained feather, loop, ladder, interlaced band, twisted chain, cable chain, rosette chain, fishbone, trellis, Cretan, Vandyke, double knot, and darning. A newcomer to embroidery, this sampler was her first attempt at crewel work.*

87 *Medallion depicting the arrival of the Normans on the English coast. From one of the long cushions in Winchester Cathedral. A detail of the supporting pattern is reproduced in illustration 80. See also illustration 78.*

Even as she plays fondly with her pipe dreams, she knows in her heart that its chances of survival are minimal; that although it is here today, pretty, fresh, and colourful, by tomorrow it will be faded and grubby, the threads worn and the colours faded; and that because the present sets very little store by its immediate past, the next generation is as likely to destroy as to cherish it. Perhaps she will comfort herself with the thought that, like a garden, much of embroidery's charm lies in the fact that it is completely ephemeral.

But to finish one piece of work is only an excuse to begin another, the idea for which she has been turning over in her mind for a long while. She cannot wait to get on with it for she is irresistibly fascinated by the art of working intricate stitches and by the variety of decorative effects she can obtain with them; by watching a design develop along the lines and in the colours she has chosen for it; and by the knotty little problems she is constantly being called upon to resolve. Absorbed in bringing into focus all her technical expertise, taste, and ingenuity, and balancing them on the point of her needle, she has neither regret nor hesitation. The past and the future may take care of themselves. Time becomes meaningless. Only the embroidery she is engaged upon at the present moment is important.

88 Mary Hancock worked this motif, based on one of Arthur H Lee & Sons' patterns, in Appleton's crewel wools, numbers 141–143, 181, 331–335, 341, 601–606, 691–693, 701, 987, 991–992.

Stitch samplers

In needle workes there doth great knowledge rest,
A fine conceit thereby full soone is shown:
A drowsie braine this skill cannot digest,
Paines spent in such, in vaine awaie is throne:
They must be careful, diligent and wise,
In needle workes that beare awaie the prise.

William Barley, 1596

There is nothing fanciful about the names of the traditional methods of embroidery. Like the techniques themselves they are practical and self-explanatory: *canvas work* in which the background as well as the pattern is covered with stitches, takes it name from the even-weave linen or canvas on which they are worked; *cut work, pulled work, drawn thread work, applied work* and *quilting* are all words that describe the action involved in performing the method; *black work* and *white work* are obviously named after the colour of the thread; *gold work* after its metallic quality. Only *crewel work* takes its name from the thread itself. No matter how the word is spelt, and there have been several variants on it, or whether it is used in the singular or plural, *crewel* is a collective noun and has always been associated with colour. Because of the innumerable textures and tones she can create with them, there are always crewel wools in the embroiderer's work bag.

The embroiderer is a connoisseur of stitches. Studying them with minute attention she realises that the distinctive character of each one depends entirely upon the angle at which she sets her needle, and the way in which she winds her thread around it.

Quickly she discovers that the tension at which she works a stitch is a matter of supreme importance. If she pulls the thread too tightly it will be hard and insensitive. If it is too loose the stitch will be unsightly and deformed. She has to find the happy medium. In her search for it she unknowingly improves her technique and begins to develop her personal style. No two embroiderers work at the same tension. Their technique is therefore measurably, though almost imperceptibly, different.

If she is wise, the embroiderer will practise each stitch until she can work it to perfection. Having mastered it, it then becomes her willing and obedient slave. The samplers she makes are her personal dictionary of stitches. They remind her not only of how each one is made, but also of the particular effect it produces. When in doubt as to which will best suit her particular purpose, she turns up her samplers and broods over them. Experience teaches her that not all stitches combine happily together, and that the same stitch worked in two or three different colours may look quite different.

The majority of stitches are astonishingly simple. Some are adaptations of the familiar stitches of fine sewing, like running and double running stitch, darning and buttonhole stitch. Others are more elaborate and complicated. Some must be worked in two separate stages, movements, or journeys, and these the embroiderer calls composite stitches.

She sees that her stitches fall naturally into groups or families. Some are flat and smooth; others are chained, crossed, knotted, looped, and interlaced. She finds that there are sometimes two apparently equally successful ways of working the same stitch. Conscientiously she tries to discover which is the correct way, for understandably she feels this must be the best way. Some say one thing, some another—who is she to believe? Obsessed with a passion for rules and regulations, the Victorian schoolmistress proliferated much unhappiness by insisting that right is right and wrong is wrong. One of the great experts on stitches, Louisa Pesel, who by studying old embroideries was able to recover from the past the secret of how many forgotten stitches were worked, disagreed with her. 'Personally,' she wrote, 'I never consider that a stitch is a good and useful stitch, or that I have discovered the right way of working it, if, after a little practice I do not find it pleasant and easy to do. So long as the front and back look exactly like the model, so long as the silk twists and interlaces in the same manner, it does not seem as if it could matter in which way it is worked.'

Respectful of her judgement in this important matter, the Keeper of Textiles in the Victoria and Albert Museum invited Louisa Pesel in 1910 to work a series of stitch samplers for the benefit of students who visited the Textile Study Rooms. Perhaps a little faded, but with the needle she used to work each one still in place, almost as though she expected to come back at any moment and pick it up again, they are still there—the definitive guide to the stitches of crewel work and to all the other methods used by English embroiderers.

The idea that the wrong side of the work must be as neat as the right is another legacy from the Victorian schoolmistress. Desirable as this may be in certain circumstances, there is little or no evidence to show that it was a precept heeded by Elizabethan and Stuart embroiderers. On the contrary, anybody who has had an opportunity to inspect the wrong side of a crewel work curtain or a work bag must instantly be struck by the fact that the frankness, urgency, and honesty of the stitchery on the front is reflected in a corresponding tangle of disorderly threads on the back. The truth is that when the embroiderer is stirred and excited by her invention, she has no time to worry about the side she sees only when she turns over her frame to make sure that each thread is run in properly and finished off securely.

With a design that pleases her and the stitches moving smoothly backwards and forwards across it, she is likely to think that rules—though they may on occasion have their uses—are made only to be broken.

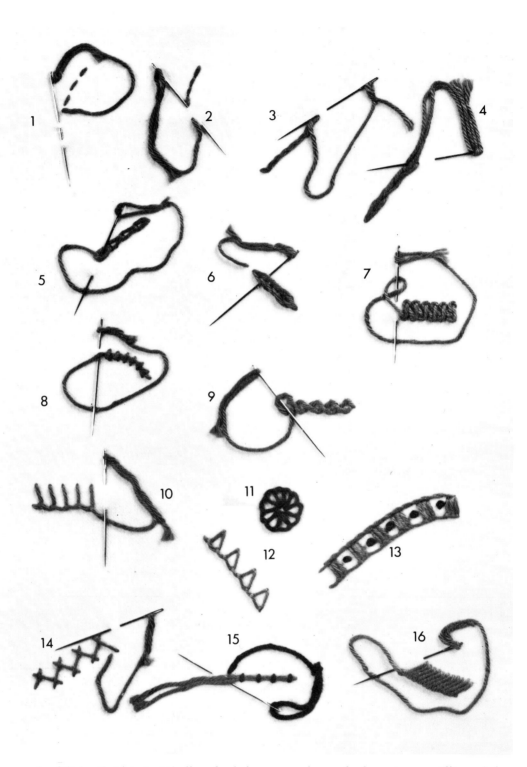

89 Stitches that interpret the line of a design: 1 running; 2 back; 3 stem; 4 split; 5 chain; 6 heavy chain; 7 braid; 8 coral; 9 link; 10 open buttonhole; 11 closed buttonhole; 12 grouped buttonhole; 13 composite stitch of stem, buttonhole, and French knots; 14 herringbone; 15 couching; 16 rope.

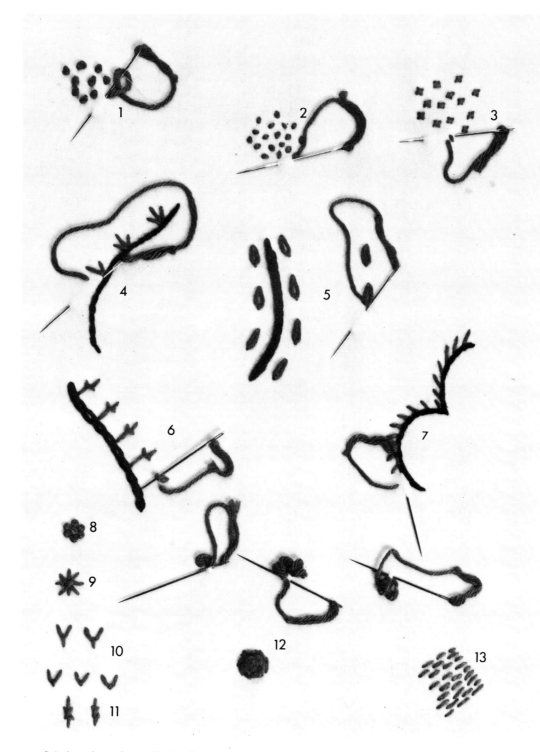

90 Stitches that give a light effect: *1 French knots; 2 seeding or speckling; 3 cross; 4 composite stitch of stem and straight; 5 detached chain or loop; 6 sword; 7 stroke; 8 French knots; 9 star; 10 fly; 11 ermine; 12 raised or plaited knots or raised rose stitch; 13 darning.*

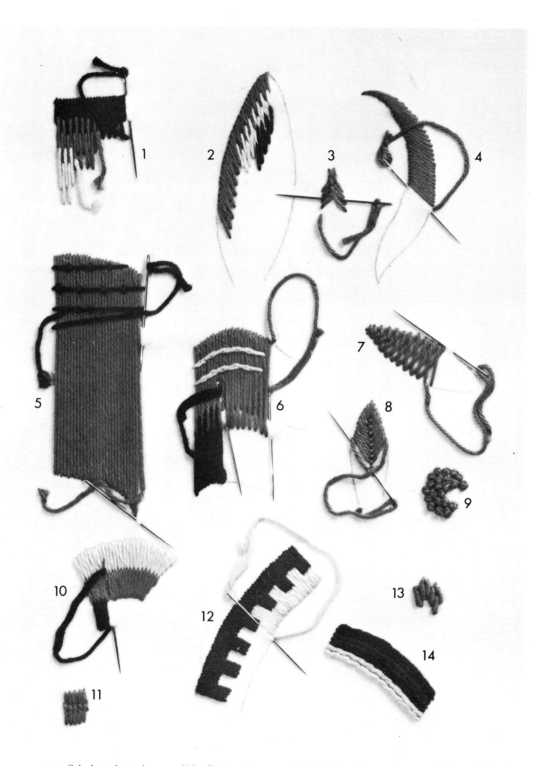

91 *Stitches that give a solid effect: 1 long and short (basic); 2 long and short (showing direction); 3 Vandyke; 4 satin; 5 laid, tied down with couching; 6 laid long and short, tied down with split stitch; 7 double back; 8 solid fly; 9 French knots; 10 encroaching satin; 11 Roumanian; 12 brick; 13 bullion knots; 14 rows of stem.*

92 *Decorative fillings: 1 basic cross bar or trellis; 2 cross bar with small diagonal stitches to hold it in position; 3 cross bar with large cross tie-down stitches; 4 cross bar with long radiating tie-down stitches and alternate squares filled with diagonal satin stitch; 5 square and diagonal cross bars, long straight tie-down stitches, and French knots; 6 solid laid held in place with plain cross bar filling; 7 variation of cross bar, with radiating short tie-down stitches and small cross stitch in centre of diamonds; 8 shaded cross bar commencing with basic cross bar filling in the darkest shade, with the next shade laid above and to the right, and only the lightest shade tied down; 9 laid leaf shape held in place with plain cross bar.*

To create a design

The long and varied tradition of English crewel embroidery has been influenced by designs and ideas from many parts of the world and, in turn, English pattern books, hangings, and samplers travelled across the Atlantic to form the foundation of American crewel work. This book has been written to show how that foundation began and developed through the centuries. But it has also been designed to be used as a practical source of patterns and techniques for beginner and expert alike.

The forty colour illustrations show a remarkable variety of form and style —the simple, vigorous commentary of the Bayeux Tapestry, the elaborate, complex symbolism of Jacobean hangings, the light flowers of the eighteenth century, right up to present-day adaptations. There are photographs of entire pieces, so you can see how small sections are combined to make up larger designs: use a magnifying glass to see the fine detail which will help you plan your own adaptation. Other pictures are shown in close-up where the colours and stitch patterns are particularly exciting.

In addition, many of the photographs are followed by drawings of individual motifs. These act as patterns for you to transfer, adapt, and arrange as you like for creating your own designs. The samplers on pages 218–221 are made up of the basic crewel stitches used in the illustrated pieces, and the needles have been left in place so that the work method is clearly visible. Below is a stitch key for the drawings, and instructions on how to enlarge (or reduce) a design are given opposite.

herringbone

long and short

rope

seeding (speckling)

French knot and plaited knot (raised rose)

stem and chain

coral

buttonhole

running

satin

stitch direction

To enlarge a design

One of the objects of this book is to provide the embroiderer with a collection of motifs, each of which is complete in itself. They can be used alone or in combination with several others, but in either case the embroiderer may want to enlarge the motifs she chooses. This is no bad thing, for the earliest crewel work patterns were not small, and stitches worked in crewel wools do not show to their best advantage if they are crowded together in too confined a space.

One way of achieving this is to use a photostat enlarger, but for those not fortunate enough to have access to one, an alternative method is given here. The diagrams overleaf show how, by covering a motif with a grid of half-inch squares, it can be enlarged by transferring it—square by square—to a grid composed of one-inch squares. The immediate result is to double the size of the motif. It can of course be made even bigger by increasing the size of the squares on the larger grid.

This method has been known to decorative artists for many centuries. Richard Shorleyker, in the pattern book he published at the beginning of the seventeenth century called *A Schole-House for the Needle,* provided the embroiderers he no doubt hoped would buy his book with two grids by means of which they could enlarge his birds, insects, fish, and flowers.

Embroiderers who wish to enlarge a motif are advised to use a ruler, sharp pencil, and good quality tracing paper, and to

First :   make an accurate tracing of each grid.
Second :   lay the smaller grid over the motif.
Third :   trace the motif onto this grid.
Fourth :   matching square for square, copy the motif onto the larger grid.

Dramatis personae

Because of the enormously wide field covered by crewel work a number of disparate characters have contributed to its history. There they all are, one after another, in the centre of the stage, a galaxy of talent, each making his or her special contribution to the whole. But not all are famous names. Certainly many are totally unknown to the embroiderer, who even if she has heard of some (and who has not?), may be quite unfamiliar with the details of their lives. So it has seemed important to include what might be called a few programme notes in which some of the participants in the drama that has been presented are allowed to explain themselves.

Boler, James

Printer. 1613 took up freedom in the Stationers' Company. 1625 acquired business formerly owned by John Hodgets at *The Marigold* in St Paul's church-yard. 1634 published *The Needle's Excellency* with introductory poem by John Taylor, who called himself The Water Poet. The patterns come chiefly from a pattern book published in Nürnberg in 1591 by Johann Sibmacher.

Burne-Jones, Edward 1833-98

Painter and designer, mainly self-taught. Set up house in Red Lion Square with William Morris and in 1860 married Georgiana Macdonald. 1861 founder member of the firm of Morris, Marshall, Faulkner & Company for which he designed tiles, tapestries, stained glass, embroideries, etc for remainder of his life. Drew book illustrations for the Kelmscott Press. 1863 Fellow of the Royal Society of Portrait Painters. 1885 Associate of Royal Academy of Arts. 1894 created baronet.

> *Memorials of Edward Burne-Jones*, Georgiana Burne-Jones (1904; USA, Richard West 1971).
>
> *History of the Royal Academy 1768-1968*, Sydney C. Hutchinson (Chapman & Hall 1968).

Crane, Walter 1845-1915

Designer, painter, book illustrator, embroidery designer, and writer on art. At age of 17 exhibited at the Royal Academy and in 1873 illustrated his first book. 1883 joined the Socialist League. Worked for Morris & Co. and the Kelmscott Press. Promoter and first president of the Art Workers' Guild. With one short gap, was president of the Arts and Crafts Exhibition Society from 1888-1919. 1898 Principal of Royal College of Art.

Day, Lewis Foreman 1845-1910

Decorative artist. 1870 set up in private practice in London as designer. Promoter with Crane and Morris of the Arts and Crafts Society and the Art Workers' Guild of which he became master. From 1897 until his death was member of council of the Royal Society of Arts. 1890 Government Inspector in painting and ornament. 1909 member of commission to advise on arrangement of collections in Victoria and Albert Museum. 1900 published *Art in Needlework* with assistance of Mary Buckle.

Evelyn, John 1620-1706

b. Wotton, Surrey, and at age of 4 attended school held in room above porch of Wotton church. 1637 admitted student of the Middle Temple, subsequently becoming a commoner of Balliol College, Oxford. On outbreak of Civil War spent a brief period in Royalist army. 1644 travelled in Europe and on return made etchings from his sketches. 1662 his name appears on founding charter of the Royal Society of which became secretary in 1772. 1664 appointed commissioner for sick and wounded survivors of Dutch Wars. 1681 consulted on founding of Chelsea Hospital and in 1695 laid foundation stone of Greenwich Hospital becoming its treasurer. 1699 on death of elder brother succeeded to the title. Splendid monument in Wotton church with wife and family.

Gerard, John 1545-1611/12?

Herbalist and apothecary. b. Nantwich, Cheshire. Studied medicine and travelled abroad, possibly as ship's surgeon. By 1577 settled in neighbourhood of Holborn. Superintendent of Lord Burleigh's garden in the Strand and at Theobalds. 1595 member of Barber-Surgeons' Company and in 1608 became master. 1596 issued list of plants he cultivated in his garden. 1596 published *The Historie of Plants*. 1633 an amended version by Thomas Johnson was issued. Buried St Andrews church, Holborn.

> *Gerard's Herball*, Marcus Woodward (ed.) (Minerva Press 1971).
> *Leaves from Gerard's Herball*, Marcus Woodward (ed.) (USA, Dover 1969).

Hogarth, Mary c. 1865-1935

b. Barton-on-Humer, Lincolnshire. Studied at Slade School of Art. Exhibited with New English Art Club. For 17 years taught at Wycombe Abbey School. Published three portfolios of topographical subjects: *Scenes in Athens, Sketches in Moorish Spain*, and *Fountains of Rome*. 1925 at request of Mrs Lewis F. Day revised *Art in Needlework*, re-writing the chapter on white work and adding one on modern trends in embroidery. 1929 revised Day's *Nature and Ornament*. Active and progressive member of the Embroiderers' Guild, contributing many articles to *Embroidery*.

Holme, Randle 1627-99

Like father and grandfather, was a genealogist, heraldic painter, and collector of manuscripts. 1688 published *The Academy of Armory and Blazon,* a book packed with information much of which is not wholly reliable. His son, the fourth Randle Home, added to manuscript collection and sold it indirectly to Robert

Harley, 1st Earl of Oxford (1661–1724), grandson of Lady Brilliana Harley. 1573 collection acquired for the nation by British Museum. Known as the Harleian Collection.

> *Prince of Librarians: Antonio Panizzi,* Edward Miller (Andre Deutch 1967; USA, Ohio University Press).

Jekyll, Gertrude 1843–1935

Grew up in Surrey. Studied at South Kensington School of Art. Knew Ruskin and Willian Morris whose work she greatly admired, and was enthusiastic supporter of the Arts and Crafts Movement. When failing eyesight forced her to give up embroidery, painting, etc., returned to Surrey and began to design gardens in the 'natural' style advocated by William Robinson. Became close friend of Edwin Lutyens (1869–1944) whose keen interest in traditional crafts-manship she shared. Wrote many books on garden design.

> *Miss Jekyll: Portrait of a Great Gardener,* Betty Massingham (Country Life 1966; USA, David & Charles 1973).
>
> 'Landscape with Flowers, West Surrey', Mavis Batey, *Garden History Society,* II, 2, 1974.

Kay-Shuttleworth, The Hon Rachel 1886–1967

While still a schoolgirl became interested in embroidery and lacemaking. Studied art in Paris, and during her extensive travels on the Continent and in North Africa, laid foundation of her notable collection of embroidery and lace. In order to gain professional expertise in needlework she sewed for a time in the workrooms of Pontings, a then fashionable store in Kensington. Began teaching and lecturing. Intensely interested in social welfare, she set up Infant Welfare Centres in Lancashire. Also played prominent part in the Girl Guide movement and in the formation of the Civic Arts Association. 1934 appointed Justice of the Peace. 1949 decorated with MBE. Vice-President of Embroiderers' Guild (1956), and contributed useful series of articles on lace to *Embroidery.* A deeply religious woman, she devoted the latter part of her life to founding a study centre for embroiderers at Gawthorpe Hall, which she endowed not only with her own collection but also with her library of books on art history. Lived long enough to know that her plans for it would be amply fulfilled.

> *Rachel Kay-Shuttleworth, a Memoir,* G. A. Williams, 1968 (obtainable from Gawthorpe Hall, Padiham, Lancashire).
>
> 'Embroidery in the Twentieth Century', Elsie Eraut, *Embroidery,* II, 1934.

Linwood, Mary 1756–1845

b. Birmingham. When she was 9, family moved to Leicester where her mother opened a school at Belgrave Gate. 1776 and 1778 exhibited needlework pictures with Leicester Society of Artists. Came to London and, encouraged by interest of Royal Family in her work, opened exhibition at The Panthenon, Oxford Street. 1798 moved to Hanover Square Concert Rooms and 1809 to Savile House, Leicester Square. Buried St Mary's Church, Leicester, where com-memorated by memorial in south aisle.

> *Ladies' Monthly Museum,* I, 1798, p. 143

Godey's *Lady's Book,* I, 1830, p. 156
P. G. Trendall, *Embroideress,* II, 1934–35, p. 369

Macbeth, Ann 1875–1948

Embroiderer. b. Bolton. 1897 studied Glasgow School of Art. 1901 invited by Jessie Newberry to become her assistant in embroidery classes. 1910 became her successor as head of the department. Also taught bookbinding and leather work. Designed for Liberty's and other firms. Exhibited widely. 1928 retired to Lake District but continued to teach and encourage embroiderers to make own patterns.

'Ann Macbeth 1875–1948', Margaret Swain, *Embroidery,* XXV, 1, 1974.

'Appreciation of the work of Ann Macbeth', Francis Newbury, *Studio,* 1903.

Markham, Gervase 1568–1637

b. Nottinghamshire. Fought in Low Countries and rose to rank of captain. Turned to literature as easy way of making money. Something of a scholar, he knew Greek and Latin as well as French, Italian, Spanish, and probably Dutch. A practical student of agriculture, became champion of improved methods of horse breeding and racing. Owner of valuable stud and said to have imported the first Arab stallion. Industry was prodigious but books shamelessly repeat themselves and he has been called the earliest English hack writer. Buried St Giles, Cripplegate.

Morris, May 1862–1938

Designer and embroiderer. Younger daughter of William Morris from whom she received her artistic training. Designed textiles, wallpapers, and embroideries for Morris & Co. and in 1885 took over management of firm's embroidery workroom. Married briefly to Henry Halliday Sparling, a member of the editorial staff of Morris's paper *The Commonweal,* founded with object of promoting socialism. 1893 published *Decorative Needlework.* 1907 founder member of Women's Guild of Arts. 1910 made lecture tour of America. Exhibited widely and wrote many articles including a substantial study of the *opus anglicanum* (*Burlington Magazine,* VII, 1905). Died at Kelmscott Manor where spent latter years of her life.

'Memories of May Morris', Una Fielding, *William Morris Society,* II, 3, 1968.

Morris, William 1834–96

Craftsman, designer, poet, novelist, and political reformer. b. Walthamstow. 1848-56 family lived at The Water House which is now the William Morris Art Gallery. Educated Marlborough College. 1853 entered Exeter College, Oxford, and met Burne-Jones. Decided to study architecture and joined staff of G. E. Street, first in Oxford and later in London. Met Philip Webb. 1859 m. Jane Burden. 1860-65 lived at Red House, Bexleyheath. 1861 was founder of firm of Morris, Marshall, Faulkner & Co. 1865 firm acquired new premises at 26 Queen Square and in 1875 it was reorganised as Morris & Co. 1871 rented Kelmscott Manor, Lechlade, with D. G. Rossetti. 1877 moved sale and showrooms of Morris & Co. to 449 Oxford Street. Founded Society for the Protection of Ancient Buildings, and worked hard to promote its cause. 1881 Morris & Co.'s workrooms moved to Merton Abbey, Surrey. 1885 founded the Socialist League. 1891 founded the Kelmscott Press.

> *William Morris*, Philip Henderson (Thames & Hudson 1967; USA, British Book Centre).
>
> *The Work of William Morris*, Paul Thompson (Heinemann 1967)

Newberry, Jessie 1864–1948

Embroiderer and designer of stained glass, etc. b. Paisley. Travelled in Italy. Studied at Glasgow School of Art and in 1890 was awarded medal for stained glass. 1889 married Francis H. Newberry (1853–1946), principal of the school. 1894 started embroidery classes at the school for both full and part time students. Added dress design to the timetable. 1910 retired for health reasons. 1918 settled in Dorset.

> 'Mrs R. J. Newberry 1864–1948', Margaret Swain, *Embroidery*, XXIV, 4, 1973.

Pesel, Louisa Frances 1870–1947

b. Bradford. Educated Bradford Grammar School. Studied design under Lewis F. Day. Founded West Riding Needlework Association, insisting that when she taught members a new stitch they in turn must teach somebody else and return next lesson with the sample to show it was worked properly. This principle she used in training the Winchester Broderers. 1903, on Lewis Day's recommendation, appointed designer to Royal Hellenic Schools of Needlework and Laces, Athens, becoming director. Organised work centres in other parts of Greece and sold work abroad. 1908 joined Embroiderers' Guild and worked hard with Mrs Newberry, Mrs Antrobus, and others to promote its interests. 1920 became first president after war. 1912 Bradford firm of Percy Lund Humphreys, later to move to London and become associated with fine printing of modern art books, published her three portfolios of stitches. 1914–18 war provided opportunity to establish Handicraft Club for wounded soldiers. 1925 moved to Winchester. Worked kneelers and cushions with help of other embroiderers for chapel in Bishop's Palace which lead to scheme for the cathedral. Buried in the cathedral precinct. Was a frequent contributor to *Embroidery* and as well as her stitch samplers, published books on canvas work, etc.

> 'Louisa Frances Pesel 1870–1947' Laura Pesel, *Embroidery*, XIII, 1, 1962.

Rich, Barnaby *c.* 1540–*c.* 1620

Distant cousin of Lord Chancellor Rich. Wholly self-educated. Enlisted in boyhood and fought in Low Countries rising to rank of captain. Later saw service in Ireland and finally settled in neighbourhood of Dublin. Wrote pamphlets, romances, etc for popular rather than cultivated audience.

93 A contemporary variant on a traditional theme, The Chinese Phoenix 1974. Worked by Mary Thomson, a mature student at the Royal School of Needlework. Stitches include stem, back, herringbone, satin, long and short, cable chain, feather, long armed feather, Vandyke, and wheatear, with woven wheels and battlement couching.

Shorleyker, Richard *d.* 1639

Printer. Served apprenticeship with Walter Dight. In his will, in 1619, Dight gave Shorleyker and another apprentice first refusal of his 'printing house, presses and other things'. In this way Shorleyker acquired premises in Shoe Lane at The Falcon. Took up freedom in Stationers' Company. 1627 secured monopoly to print *A Schole-House for the Needle*, issuing the tenth edition in 1624. Buried St Bride's, Fleet Street.

Taylor, John 1580–1653

b. Gloucester. Failing to get place at Oxford walked to London and apprenticed himself to Thames watermen, returning to the same trade when, after service in navy, retired with wounded leg. Increased earnings by writing easy rhyming verses to order and undertaking wagering journeys—today's sponsored walks—which he announced beforehand in pamphlets he called *Taylor's Bills*. Best remembered of these pranks was his attempt to row across the Thames with a friend in boat made of oiled paper, which they propelled with oars made of cane with a fish tied to one end. 1630 published an edition of his writings called *All the Works of John Taylor, The Water Poet, being 63 in Number.*

Terry, Edward *c.* 1595–1660

b. near Penshurst, Kent. 1616 went out to India as chaplain to one of East India Company's expeditions. When Sir Thomas Roe's chaplain died, Terry was appointed to succeed him. Returned with him to England and was commended for his sober and honest life. 1629 appointed rector of Great Greenford, Middlesex, and was buried in the chancel. 1655 published *A Voyage to the East Indies.*

Traquair, Phoebe Anna 1852–1936

Studied at Dublin School of Art. 1873 married Dr R. H. Traquair, Keeper of the Natural History Department of the Museum of Science and Art, Edinburgh. Began making precise drawings of skeletal remains and other natural objects, and painted murals in various public buildings. By 1879 was designing and executing her own embroideries. Also noted for her enamel work, jewellery, book binding, and illuminated manuscripts, and by the turn of the century was recognised as one of the leading figures in the Arts and Crafts movement in Scotland.

> 'Some Early Embroideries by Mrs Phoebe Traquair', Barbara Morris, *Embroidery*, Diamond Jubilee Issue 1966.

Tusser, Thomas *c.* 1524–1580

Poet, musician, and agricultural writer. b. Rivenhall, Essex. Chorister at St Paul's Cathedral and held appointment as court musician. Settled eventually at Cattiwade, Suffolk, and introduced barley growing to the district. Died London. Buried St Mildred-in-the-poultry.

94 Sampler worked by Dorothea Nield when a student at the Royal School of Needlework. Stitches include long and short, satin, block satin, coral, heavy chain, detached chain, stem, and French knots.

Webb, Philip 1831–1915

Architect and designer. b. Oxford. 1852 became principal assistant to G. E. Street. 1858 went into private practice designing furniture, etc. Founder member of Morris, Marshall, Faulkner & Co. and designed furniture, metalwork, glass, etc. for the firm. Designed large number of country houses including Rounton Grange, Northallerton.

Young, Arthur 1741–1820

As young man known for his foppery in dress and love of dancing. Precocious child who began writing history of England when still at school. Made little money with pen and failed to achieve success until took to study of agriculture, after which his principal works were translated into several languages, and his advice was sought by both English and foreign agriculturalists. He introduced new and more scientific methods of farming in order to achieve maximum production. On death of his father went to live at Bradfield Hall, Bradfield, Suffolk, which had been part of his mother's dowry. On her death he inherited the property. Unhappily married to Martha Allen of King's Lynn, Norfolk.

The pleasures of reading about embroidery

Textile historians study embroidery academically and the end product of their research is a catalogue, a discourse to a learned society, or an article in an art historical periodical like *Apollo* or *The Burlington Magazine*. But embroiderers, although aware of the importance to them of the past, study it differently. They look at the embroiderer's techniques, stitches, and methods, at her design, and at the way in which she has reached solutions to the special problems with which she was confronted. They cannot readily put words around this experience, but it undoubtedly influences their own work. This is well illustrated by the bird worked in crewel wools [93].

The natural and pleasant consequence of studying a piece of embroidery in this way is a dawning interest in the embroiderer herself as a person, and a desire to know more about her social background, her house and garden, clothes, and furniture. So to the following bibliography of articles relevant to crewel work that have appeared in *The Embroideress* or *Embroidery* and have not been mentioned in the text, has been added a list of readily available and comparatively inexpensive books called 'The embroiderer in context'. There is also one on styles in art to help those interested in discovering why the appearance of the embroiderer's motifs, if not necessarily the motifs themselves, changes from one period to another. Each of these reliable publications contains a thoroughly useful and practical bibliography for further reading.

To these has been added a short list of books on the oriental influence on English art and one on the Bayeux Tapestry. Without leaning heavily on them, no embroiderer could begin to write about crewel work. I am personally more deeply grateful to the scholars, the results of whose research is distilled in every one of them, than they can ever know.

1 Select list of relevant articles published in *Embroidery* between 1933 and 1970

(Publication ceased during the war, after which a second series was started.)

'English Embroidery in the Sixteenth Century', A. F. Kendrick, I, 3 and 4, 1933.
'Some Sixteenth Century Pattern Books', Margaret Dowling, I, 3, 1934.
'English Embroidery of the Seventeenth Century', Frances Burlison, II, 3, 1934.
'English Embroidery of the Eighteenth Century', A. E. Mundy, II, 3, 1934.

'Indian Embroidery', A. D. Howell-Smith, III, 3, 1935.
'Traditional Chinese Embroidery', Neville Whymant, III, 4, 1935.
'Needlework in the Time of Queen Elizabeth and JamesI', John L. Nevinson, IV, 4, 1936.
'Embroideries at Blicking Hall, Norfolk', Pamela Clabburn, IV, 1, 1953.
'Needlework in the Choir of Wells Cathedral', IV, 4, 1953.
'Interesting Embroideries in Derby', Grace Bracebridge, V, 2, 1954.
'Some Embroideries at Cotehele House, Cornwall', Dorothy Stanbury, VIII, 4, 1957.
'Indo-European Embroideries', John C. Irwin, X, 1, 1959.
'Marlborough College Embroideries', Sybil Matthews, XII, 1, 1960.
'English Crewel Work Curtains in the Royal Ontario Museum', Katherine B. Brett, XVI, 1, 1965.
'The Embroideries at Gawthorpe Hall', Maisie C. Currey, XVI, 1, 1965.

2   List of relevant articles (not mentioned in the text) published in *The Embroideress* between 1922 and 1939

'Some Near Eastern Embroidery Designs', Percy E. Newberry, I, 1922–23, p. 75.
'The Royal School of Needlework', I, 1922–23, p. 166.
'Exhibition of embroidery arranged by the British Institute of Industrial Art at the Victoria and Albert Museum' (a review), I, 1922–23, p. 193, *a*.
'Colour and Stitchery', Louisa F. Pesel, II, 1924–25, p. 195 (replies on pp. 226, 263, 265, 269).
'First public exhibition of the Embroiderers' Guild' (a review), Mary Hogarth, II, 1924–25, p. 212.
'Old Manuscript Pattern Books', G. M. Hawkes, II, 1924–25, p. 300.
'A Stuart Bed Curtain', A. J. B. Wace, III, 1926–27, p. 459.
'Some Elizabethan Embroideries', A. J. B. Wace, III, 1926–27, p. 507.
Obituary: Mrs Lewis F. Day, IV, 1928–29, p. 720.
'The Yew Tree Linen Industry', Louisa F. Pesel, VI, 1932–33, p. 967.
'A St Swithun's Day Enterprise', Louisa F. Pesel, VI, 1932–33, p. 1039.
'Indian Embroidery', Kathleen Harris, VII, 1934–36, p. 1189.
'Embroideries of India', W. G. Raffe, X-XII, 1937–39, p. 1723.

3   The embroiderer in context

Houses

Great Houses of Britain, Nigel Nicolson (Weidenfeld & Nicolson 1965; USA, Putman 1965).
English Country Houses 1715 to 1760, Christopher Hussey (Country Life 1955).
Felbrigg: The Story of a House 1600 to 1960, R. W. Ketton-Cremer (Rupert Hart-Davis 1962).

Gardens and Parks

A History of British Gardening, Miles Hadfield (Hamlyn 1969).
Gerard's Herball, Marcus Woodward, ed. (Minerva Press 1971).
Leaves from Gerard's Herball, Marcus Woodward, ed. (USA, Dover 1969).
English Cottage Gardens, Edward Hyams (Nelson 1970).
English Landscaping and Literature 1660 to 1840, Edward Malins (Oxford University Press 1966).
Regent's Park, Ann Saunders (David & Charles 1969; USA, Kelly 1969).

Families and Diaries

The English Face, David Piper (Thames & Hudson 1957).

The Paston Letters, Norman Davis, ed. (UK and USA, Oxford University Press 1971).

The Cecils of Hatfield House, David Cecil (Constable 1973; USA, Houghton Mifflin 1973).

Life in a Noble Household 1641 to 1700 (The Russells of Woburn), Gladys Scott Thomson (Jonathan Cape 1965; USA, Fernhill 1950).

The Autobiography and Correspondence of Mary Granville, Mrs Delany, Rt Hon Lady Llanover, ed. (London 1862).

The Days of Duchess Anne. Life in the Household of the Duchess of Hamilton, Rosalind K. Marshall (Collins 1974).

Earls of Creation, James Lees-Milne (Hamish Hamilton 1962).

The Diary of Fanny Burney, Lewis Gibbs, ed. (Dent 1940; USA, Dutton).

The Purefoy Letters 1735 to 1753, G. Eland, ed. (Sidgwick & Jackson 1931).

Purefoy Letters 1735-1753, L. G. Mitchell, ed. (St Martin Press 1973).

The Diary of a Country Parson: The Rev James Woodforde (5 vols), James Beresford, ed. (Clarendon Press 1968).

Women in Print: Writing Women and Women's Magazines from the Restoration to 1837, Alison Adburgham (Allen & Unwin 1972; USA, Hilary House 1973).

Shopping

Shops and Shopping 1800 to 1914, Alison Adburgham (Allen & Unwin 1964).

A History of Shopping, Dorothy Davis (Routledge & Kegan Paul 1966).

Costume

Handbook of Costume, Janet Arnold (Macmillan 1974).

A History of Costume in the West, Francois Boucher (Thames & Hudson 1967).

Fashion through Fashion Plates 1771 to 1971, Doris Langley Moore (Ward Lock 1971; USA, Potter 1972).

Dress, Art and Society 1560 to 1970, Geoffrey Squire (Studio Vista 1974).

Furniture

Furniture 700 to 1700, Eric Mercer (Weidenfeld & Nicolson 1969).

English Furniture Designs of the Eighteenth Century, Peter Ward-Jackson (HMSO 1958; USA, Pendragon House 1958).

Cabinet Makers and Furniture Designers, Hugh Honour (Spring Books 1969; USA, Putman 1969).

Silver

Silver, Gerald Taylor (Cassell 1965).

Art in Silver and Gold, Gerald Taylor (Studio Vista 1964; USA, Gannon).

Glass

Glass, George Savage (Weidenfeld & Nicolson 1969).

Glass through the Ages, E. Barrington Haynes (Penguin Books 1969; USA, Gannon).

Ceramics

Pottery and Porcelain, John Cushion (The Connoisseur 1972).

Musical Instruments
Old Musical Instruments, David Hermges (Weidenfeld & Nicolson 1968).

4   Styles in art: general

Civilisation, Kenneth Clark (BBC & John Murray 1969; USA, Harper & Row 1970).
Studies in Art, Architecture and Design: vol 1, *From Mannerism to Romanticism;* vol 2, *Victorian and After*, Nikolaus Pevsner (Thames & Hudson 1969; USA, Walker & Co).
Early Medieval Art, John Beckwith (Thames & Hudson 1964; USA, Praeger 1964).
The Early Renaissance, Michael Levey (UK and USA, Penguin Books 1967).
The Seventeenth and Eighteenth Centuries, Michael Levey (Thames & Hudson 1969; USA, Dell).
Neo-Classicism, Hugh Honour (Penguin Books 1968; USA, Gannon).
The Pre-Raphaelites, Timothy Hilton (Thames & Hudson 1970; USA, Transatlantic 1973).
The Gothic Revival, Kenneth Clark (John Murray 1962; USA, Humanities Press 1970).
The World of Edwardiana, Philippe Garner (Hamlyn 1974).

5   Styles in art: the 'Oriental Style'

'Origins of the "Oriental Style" in English Decorative Art', John C. Irwin, Burlington Magazine, 97, 1955.
Indian Art, John C. Irwin (HMSO, Victoria & Albert Museum, 1969).
Origins of Chintz, John C. Irwin and Katherine B. Brett (HMSO, Victoria & Albert Museum, 1970).
'Art and the East India Trade', John C. Irwin, *J. Royal Society of Arts*, CXXX, 5191, 1972.
Chinoiserie, Hugh Honour (John Murray 1961; USA, Harper & Row 1973).

6   The Bayeux Tapestry

The Bayeux Tapestry (2nd ed.), Frank Stenton, ed. (Phaidon 1965).
The Bayeux Tapestry, C. Gibbs-Smith (UK and USA, Phaidon 1973).
'The Bayeux Tapestry and the French Secular Epic', Charles R. Dodwell, *Burlington* CVIII, 764, 1966.
'Merchants and Adventurers in India', B. G. Gokhale, *History Today*, 21, 8, 1971.

Crewel embroidery in context 1066-1900

In writing this book I have, as it were, drawn a vertical line through roughly eight hundred years of history. Across this very long period of time I have now ruled a number of horizontal lines and recorded on them a somewhat arbitrary selection from the major historical events encompassed by it, and the names of notable men and women who have left their mark upon it. The result is plainly incomplete. In terms of crewel work it is no more than a lattice of carefully laid threads which the embroiderer, following the example of Abigail Pett, can embellish with her own filling stitches. For easy reference the majority of the entries have been collected from Professor G. M. Trevelyan's *History of England* and Sir Kenneth Clark's *Civilisation*, the best of all companions for anyone in search of an introduction to the great styles in art which, through the ages, have influenced embroidery patterns. The notes on embroidery, tapestry and lace have come largely from Patricia Wardle's *Guide to English Embroideries in the Victoria and Albert Museum*, G. W. Thomson's *History of Tapestry*, and Mrs Bury Palliser's invaluable *History of Lace*. I am grateful to all those who have helped with the exacting task and in particular to Mrs Audrey Bevis who planned the lay-out. This history chart appears on the following six pages.

MONARCHS	EVENTS	PEOPLE
The Normans	1087 Domesday Survey	Lanfranc of Caen, Archbishop of
	1164 Constitutions of Clarendon define boundaries of	Canterbury
1066–1087 William the	Church and State	Thomas of Bayeux, Archbishop of York
Conqueror	*c* 1179 Trial by jury established	1118–1170 Thomas à Becket
1087–1100 William II	1196 First crusade	
1100–1135 Henry I	Court of Exchequer founded	
1135–1154 Stephen	See of York subordinated to Canterbury	
The Plantagenets		
1154–1189 Henry II		
1189–1199 Richard I		

MONARCHS	EVENTS	PEOPLE
1199–1216 John	Crusades continue	1181–1226 St Francis of Assisi
1216–1272 Henry III	Mendicant friars	1200–1259 Kublai Khan
1272–1307 Edward I	Lord Chancellor becomes Chief Minister of England	1200–1259 Matthew Paris
1307–1327 Edward II	Universities at Paris, Bologna, Salamanca, etc.	1227–1274 St Thomas Aquinas
1327–1377 Edward III	Universities of Oxford and Cambridge established	1227–1274 Marco Polo
1377–1399 Richard II	1215 Magna Carta	1240–1302 Cimabue
	1253 Death of Black Prince	1240–1330 Giovanni Pisano
	1277 Earliest dated English memorial brass	1265–1321 Dante Alighieri
	Beginning of modern statute law	1267–1337 Giotto
	1332 Parliament divided into two houses	1304–1374 Petrarch
	1337 Outbreak of Hundred Years War	*c* 1329–1384 John Wycliffe
	Black Death	*c* 1330–*c*1400 William Langland
	1340 First European paper mill built	*c* 1340–1400 Geoffrey Chaucer
	1346 Battle of Crècy	*c* 1366–1426 Jan van Eyck
	1381 Peasants' Revolt	
	1383 John Wycliffe's translation of part of the Bible	
	Winchester College founded by William of Wykeham	
	1399 English becomes language of Parliament	

MONARCHS	EVENTS	PEOPLE
House of Lancashire	1431 Death of Joan of Arc	1377–1446 Brunelleschi
	Eton College founded by Henry VI	1378–1455 Ghiberti
1399–1413 Henry IV	1453 Battle of Agincourt, English expelled from France	1383–1466 Donatello
1413–1422 Henry V	and end of Hundred Years War	1389–1464 Cosimo de' Medici
1422–1461 Henry VI	1455 Outbreak of Wars of the Roses	1401–1428 Masaccio
	1476 Caxton sets up printing press in London	1416–1492 Piero della Francesca
	Spanish Inquisition	1430–1516 Giovanni Bellini
House of York	1488 Bartholomew Dias de Noaves sails round Cape of	1444–1514 Bramante
	Good Hope	1444–1510 Botticelli
1461–1483 Edward IV	1492 Christopher Columbus discovers American	1448–1492 Lorenzo de' Medici
1483 Edward V	continent	1452–1519 Leonardo da Vinci
1483–1485 Richard III	1492 Moors finally driven out of Spain	1460–1524 Hans Holbein the Elder
1485–1509 Henry VII	1497 London Law Library founded	1466–1536 Erasmus
	1498 Vasco da Gama discovers sea route to India	1469–1527 Machiavelli
		1471–1528 Albrecht Dürer

MONARCHS	EVENTS	PEOPLE
House of Tudor	1513 Battle of Flodden	1475–1564 Michelangelo
	1520 Magellan sails round Cape Horn	1477–1510 Giorgione
1509–1547 Henry VIII	1527 Sack of Rome	1478–1535 Sir Thomas More
1547–1553 Edward VI	1529–1536 Reformation	1483–1520 Raphael

1050 Work begins on church of St Etienne, Caen, founded by William the Conqueror

Romanesque cathedrals at Canterbury, Durham, Ely, Exeter, Gloucester, Norwich, Peterborough, St Albans, Winchester, Worcester, York

1078 Chapel in Tower of London

Cathedrals in Europe at Angoulême, Autun, Compostella, Lund, Speyer, Vézelay, etc

1137-1150 Leaning Tower of Pisa

Development of art of stained glass

Notable schools of manuscript illuminators

Anglo-Saxon liveliness: Bayeux Tapestry, the earliest surviving example of English secular embroidery

Solemnity of the Romanesque: stole and maniple of St Cuthbert worked 909–916 (Durham Cathedral)

2 fragments from tomb of William of St Carilee worked 1060–1090 (Durham Cathedral). Pattern includes motifs similar to those on borders of Bayeux Tapestry

Maniple and apparel of an amice worked between 1040 and 1070; part of set of vestments traditionally supposed to have been used by Thomas à Becket during his exile in France 1164 to 1170 (Sens Cathedral)

Development of the art of tapestry weaving

1180–1210 Mitres depicting martyrdom of Thomas à Becket

1190–1220 The Worcester fragments

1220-1266 Salisbury Cathedral built

Cathedrals in Europe at Arles, Augsburg, Bayeux, Chartres, Cluny, Fontevrault, Montreale, Pisa, Sta Sophia, Siena, Toledo, Trogir, Tournai, etc

Castles at Dover, Harlech, etc

Paris centre of book illumination

English illuminators produce the Lambeth and Winchester Bibles, Benedictional of St Ethelwold, etc

1379 Wilton Dyptych (National Gallery)

Art of fresco painting developed in Italy

Beginning of musical notation

Troubadours of Provence

Clavichord begins long period of popularity

Rules of perspective formulated

Establishment of libraries

Publication of Langland's *Piers Ploughman* and Chaucer's *Canterbury Tales*

Gothic grace and naturalism: *c* 1250-1350 Great period of *opus anglicanum*

International reputation of English embroiderers at its height

1272-1294 Clare Chasuble (Victoria and Albert Museum)

1300–1320 Syon Cope and John of Thanet panel (Victoria and Albert Museum)

1315-1335 Bologna and Pienza Copes

1330–1340 Leopards of England (Musée de Cluny, Paris)

1330–1350 Chichester-Constable Chasuble (Cloisters, New York)

1340–1370 Lateran and Vich Copes

Coat armour of the Black Prince (Canterbury Cathedral)

Foundation of high warp tapestry factories in Paris, Arras, Tournai, etc

c 1379 Nicolas Bataille weaves Apocalypse tapestries (Angers) for Duke of Anjou

c 1385 Nine Heroes tapestries (Cloisters, New York)

Workshops produce Arras thread and Cyprus (gold) thread

Buildings: Westminster Hall, Eton College Chapel, Beauchamp Chapel, St George's Chapel (Windsor), etc

Alabaster tombs and memorial brasses

1419 Work begins on new facade of St Mark's, Venice, preceded by building of Palace of Doges

1453 Turks capture Constantinople; Byzantine Empire ends

Beginning of Italian Renaissance

Development of oil painting in Italy

Brunelleschi and Ghiberti at work on Duomo, Florence

Piero della Francesca's painting of ideal Renaissance town

Burgundian School of Music

Les Très Riches Heures du Duc de Berry

Malory's *Morte d'Arthur*

Everyman and the Mystery Plays

1492 Château at Ambroise built for Charles VIII

Embroiderers begin to adopt mass production methods and abandon traditional technique of underside couching

Innumerable detached motifs worked and applied to vestments, coat armour, etc

More elaborate figure compositions confined to orphreys

c 1425-1450 Chatsworth Hunting tapestries (Victoria and Albert Museum)

c 1450 figures become bulky and draperies heavy and angular

1470-1509 Stonyhurst vestments

c 1480–1490 La Dame à la Licorne tapestry (Musée de Cluny, Paris)

1490-1512 Pall of Merchant Taylors' Company

1490-1538 Fayrey Pall (Dunstable Priory, Bedfordshire)

Palls of Brewers' and Fishmongers' Companies

Lace mentioned in royal accounts

Buildings: Henry VII's Chapel, King's College Chapel, Bath Abbey, Great Hall (Hampton Court), Palace of Nonsuch, Blickling Hall, Comptom Wynyates, Hardwick Hall, Parham Park, Wollaton Hall

c 1500 Gold lace made in Venice

1515-1519 *Acts of the Apostles* tapestries woven at Brussels from cartoons by Raphael

1527 Peter Quentel publishes pattern book in Leipzig

MONARCHS	EVENTS	PEOPLE
House of Tudor (cont'd)	1535 First complete version of the Bible in English	1483–1546 Luther
	1536–1540 Dissolution of the monasteries	1488–1568 Miles Coverdale
1553–1558 Mary	1540 First Book of Common Prayer	*c* 1495–1546 Giulio Romano
1558–1603 Elizabeth I	*c* 1550 Beginning of the Counter-Reformation	1497/8–1543 Hans Holbein the Younger
	1554 Mary marries Philip of Spain	1500–1571 Benvenuto Cellini
	1561 Mary Queen of Scots returns to Scotland	1509–1564 John Calvin
	1572 Massacre of St Bartholomew's Day	1510–1580 Palladio
	Voyages of Drake, Hawkins, Raleigh, etc	1511–1574 Vasari
	1587 Execution of Mary Queen of Scots	*c* 1513–1572 John Knox
	1590 Invention of the telescope	1520–1598 William Cecil
	Invention of the camera obscura	*c* 1525–1594 Palestrina
	Growing power of House of Commons	1541–1614 El Greco
		1543–1623 William Byrd
		1546–1616 Shakespeare
		1547–1616 Cervantes
		1547–1619 Nicholas Hilliard
		1552–1599 Edmund Spenser
		1557–*c* 1603 Thomas Morley
		1561–1633 Jacopo Peri
		1563–1612 Robert Cecil
		1564–1642 Galileo
		1566–1617 Isaac Oliver
		1567–1643 Monteverdi
		1570–1650 Titian
		1573–1654 William Laud
		1573–1652 Inigo Jones
		1577–1640 Rubens

House of Stuart	1600 East India Company incorporated	1593–1625 Georges de la Tour
	1605 Gunpowder Plot	1593–1641 Thomas Wentworth, Earl of Strafford
1603–1625 James I	1607 Sir Walter Raleigh founds Virginia	1593/4–1665 Nicolas Poussin
1625–1649 Charles I	1618 Outbreak of Thirty Years War	1598–1680 Bernini
(1649–1660 The Commonwealth)	1620 Pilgrim Fathers	1599–1641 Sir Anthony van Dyck
	1628 Petition of Rights	1599–1660 Velasquez
1660–1685 Charles II	Increase in adherents to Nonconformist Churches	1600–1682 Claude Lorrain
1685–1688 James II	1642–46 Civil War	1606–1669 Rembrandt
1689–1694 William III and (until 1694) Mary	1643 Louis XIV King of France	1608–1674 John Milton
	Taxation imposed only by Act of Parliament	1609–1674 Edward Hyde, Earl of Clarendon
	1660 Restoration of monarchy	1613–1700 André le Nôtre
	1660 Founding of Royal Society	1618–1683 J-B Colbert
	Earl of Clarendon becomes Lord Chancellor	1619–1690 Charles le Brun
	Clarendon Code	1628–1688 John Bunyan
	1662 Authorised version of Bible	1632–1704 John Locke
	1662 Act of Uniformity	1632–1675 Vermeer
	1665 Great Plague	1632–1723 Sir Christopher Wren
	1666 Great Fire of London	1633–1703 Samuel Pepys
	1667 Founding of Académie des Sciences, Paris	1639–1699 Racine
	1673 Test Act	1642–1727 Sir Isaac Newton
	1675 Greenwich Royal Observatory	1656–1742 Sir Edmund Halley*
	1685 Louis XIV revokes edict of Nantes	
	1688 Glorious (Bloodless) Revolution	

* Halley's Comet appears on the Bayeux Tapestry

THE ARTS

Renaissance buildings in Europe: Château at Chenenceaux; Francis I makes additions to château at Blois, builds Chambord, Fontainebleau, etc
1506 Foundation laid of new St Peter's, Rome
1508 Michelangelo begins work on ceiling in Sistine Chapel
1521 Earliest dated harpsichord
Lute, virginals and madrigals popular
Pavane and Galliard popular dances
Morris dancers
1527 Piazza at Venice re-planned
1536 Holbein the Younger court painter to Henry VIII
1546 Palace of the Louvre begun
1550 Palladio publishes his *Four Books of Architecture*
1550 Vasari publishes his *Lives of the Painters*, etc
1551-1587 Conrad Gesner's *Historia Animalium* published
Botany becomes a science
Publication of books on gardening, herbals, florilegia, etc
Development of art of garden design
English School of Miniature Painters
Limoges enamels
Autobiography of the goldsmith Benvenuto Cellini
First London theatres built
1563 Philip of Spain builds El Escorial
c 1570 Palladio designs Villa Rotonda (Vicenza)
1571 Cosimo de' Medici completes Laurentian library (Florence)
Vasari builds Uffizi Palace for Cosimo de' Medici
1597 Morley publishes *Plaine and Easie Introduction to Practicall Musicke*

Buildings: Castle Howard, Chatsworth, Clandon, Greenwich Hospital (now Royal Naval College), Hampton Court, Hatfield House, Wilton House, The Vyne
Inigo Jones introduces Renaissance architecture at Banqueting House (Whitehall), Queen's House (Greenwich), St Paul's (Covent Garden), etc
1607 First performance of Monteverdi's *Orpheus*
1635 Rubens paints ceiling of Banqueting House
Louis XIV builds Versailles and le Nôtre lays out gardens
1642 Rembrandt paints *The Night Watch*
Inigo Jones, Ben Jonson, etc devise masques for English court
Development of ballet
1651 John Playford publishes *The English Dancing Master*
1661 Lely court painter to Charles II
1662 le Brun court painter to Louis XIV
1666 Beauchamps pioneers dance notation and becomes director of Académie Royale de Masque, Paris
Introduction of spinet; development of chamber music, opera and oratorio
Comedia dell'Arte in Italy
Lavish garden designs; fashion for plant collecting; 'tulipomania'

EMBROIDERY, TAPESTRY AND LACE

Professional workrooms continue and domestic embroidery reaches its High or Great period
Black work appears and is developed in England in a variety of ways, eg geometric fillings, speckling, etc
c 1530 Nicolo Zoppini and Willem Vorstermann publish pattern books, the latter in an English edition
1546 Cosimo de' Medici sets up tapestry factory in Florence
c 1550 Fashion for 'paned' or 'paled' work in applied silk or gold cords
Large scale canvas-work, eg Gifford and Bradford table carpets, valances, etc
Slips and medallions in tent or cross stitch applied to long cushions, hangings, etc
1561 Broderers' Company re-incorporated
1563 Statute of Artificers governing apprenticeship, etc
Guipure lace worn by Mary Queen of Scots
c 1570 Oxburgh Hangings
Old Testament subjects popular for pictures and long pillows
Lavish embroidery on court dress, masque costume, etc
Jackets, coifs, nightcaps, etc with coiling stems enclosing flowers
Sheldon tapestry factory founded
Invention of the stocking frame
Development of needlepoint lace and *lacis*
Publication of patterns for pillow lace
1586 Jacque le Moyne De Morgue publishes *La Clef des Champs*
Other pattern books issued by Thomas Geminus (1548) Adrian Pointz (1591) and William Barley (1597)
1598 Earliest dated English sampler by Jane Bostocke (Victoria and Albert Museum)

Continuation of style and methods of Elizabethan era
Embroidered boxes, caskets, bookcovers, mirror-frames, etc
Beadwork baskets, ornaments, etc
Samplers long and narrow with much elaborate cut-work
Revival of interest in Ecclesiastical embroidery under Archbishop Laud
Many designs adapted from engravings of Crispin de Passe
Pattern books by Mignerak (1605) and Trevelyon (1608)
1613 James I founds Mortlake tapestry factory
James I encourages planting of mulberry trees as part of plans for silk industry
Huguenot weavers and lacemakers arrive
1624 *A Schole-House for the Needle* (Shorleyker)
1633 Last literary references to black work
1634 *The Needle's Excellency* (James Boler)
History of Achilles tapestries designed by Rubens for Charles I
Edmund Harrison Chief Embroiderer to Charles I and Charles II
Development of pictorial embroidery in tent stitch, subjects chiefly biblical and mythological
c 1650-1680 Craze for stumpwork
c 1650 Red crewel wool on twill appears
c 1670 Fashion for knotting begins

MONARCHS	EVENTS	PEOPLE
	1688 Founding of Ashmolean Museum, Oxford	1658–1765 Henry Purcell
	1689 Toleration Act	1661–1731 Daniel Defoe
	1694 Founding of Bank of England	1661–1736 Nicholas Hawksmoor
	Emergence of Whig and Tory parties	1664–1726 Sir John Vanburgh
		1677–1745 Jonathan Swift
House of Stuart (cont'd)	1701 Act of Settlement	1684–1721 Watteau
	1704 Battle of Blenheim	1685–1750 Bach
1702–1714 Anne	1720 South Sea Bubble	1688–1759 Handel
	1721–1742 Robert Walpole Prime Minister	1692–1764 Hogarth
	1745–1746 Jacobite Rebellion	1697–1768 Canaletto
House of Hanover	1746 Battle of Culloden Moor	1709–1784 Samuel Johnson
	1748–1756 War of the Austrian succession	1712–1778 Rousseau
1714–1727 George I	1757 Pitt the Elder leader of Tory party	1727–1788 Thomas Gainsborough
1727–1760 George II	1759 Quebec captured from French	1728–1792 Robert Adam
1760–1820 George III*	*c* 1760–1820 Industrial Revolution	1730–1795 Josiah Wedgwood
	Discovery of steam power	1732–1809 Haydn
	Building of canals	1746–1828 Goya
	John Wesley establishes Methodism	1749–1832 Goethe
	1773 Boston Tea Party followed by outbreak of	1756–1791 Mozart
	American War of Independence	1759–1796 Robert Burns
	1774 Cook explores coast of New Zealand	1769–1852 Duke of Wellington
	1776 Declaration of American Independence	1770–1827 Beethoven
	Increasing power of landed gentry	1770–1850 Wordsworth
	1783 Pitt the Younger Prime Minister	1771–1837 Sir Walter Scott
	1789 French Revolution	1775–1817 Jane Austen
	1793 Execution of Louis XVI and Marie Antoinette	1775–1851 Turner
	1798 Battle of the Nile	1776–1837 Constable
1820–1830 George IV	1803–1815 Napoleonic Wars	1788–1824 Byron
1830–1837 William IV	1804 Founding of the Horticultural Society	1795–1881 Thomas Carlyle
	1805 Battle of Trafalgar	1797–1828 Schubert
	1807 Abolition of slavery	1798–1863 Delacroix
House of Windsor	1813 Monopoly of East India Company abolished	1809–1892 Tennyson
	1815 Battle of Waterloo	1810–1856 Schumann
1837–1901 Victoria	1831 Covent Garden Market built	1810–1849 Chopin
	1832 Reform Bill	1811–1886 Liszt
	Beginning of the Oxford Movement	1812–1870 Charles Dickens
	1838 First steam ship crosses Atlantic	1813–1883 Wagner
	Brunel builds Clifton Suspension Bridge; Doebling	1816–1855 Charlotte Brontë
	builds Brooklyn Bridge	1819–1900 John Ruskin
	c 1840 Invention of the camera	1822–1910 William Holman Hunt
	c 1840 First prefabricated buildings	1828–1882 Dante Gabriel Rossetti
	1844 Publication of Engels' *Conditions of the Working*	1828–1910 Tolstoy
	Classes in England	1829–1896 Millais
	1848 Public Health Act	1832–1883 Edouard Manet
	1851 Great Exhibition	1833–1897 Brahms
	1854–1856 Crimean War	1834–1896 William Morris
	1857 Indian Mutiny	1834–1903 Whistler
	1865 General Booth founds the Salvation Army	1839–1906 Cézanne
	1870 Education Act	1840–1917 Rodin
	1871 Franco-Prussian War	1841–1919 Renoir
	1871 Trades Union Act	1848–1903 Gauguin
	1877 Victoria assumes title of Empress of India	1853–1890 van Gogh
	1899–1902 South African War	1857–1934 Sir Edward Elgar
		1872–1898 Aubrey Beardsley

* 1811–1820 Regency

THE ARTS	EMBROIDERY, TAPESTRY AND LACE
Wren builds Sheldonian Theatre (Oxford), Pembroke and Emmanuel Colleges (Cambridge), etc. 1675-1710 Wren rebuilds St Paul's Cathedral and Grinling Gibbons carves choir stalls, etc Hawksmoor builds west front of Westminster Abbey	Colbert founds tapestry factories of Gobelins (1662) and Beauvais (1664) 1689 Soho tapestry factory 1696 Earliest dated crewel work hangings (Royal Ontario Museum, Toronto)
Buildings: Althorp, Blenheim, Brighton Pavillion, Chiswick House, Holkham, Kedleston, Kenwood, Mellerstein, Osterley, Syon House, Stowe, Strawberry Hill, The Mansion House *The Tatler, Spectator, Gentlemen's Magazine, Ladies' Magazine,* etc appear 1702-1717 Kneller paints members of the Kit Cat Club *c* 1709 Invention of the pianoforte Beginning of the symphony in contemporary form 1715 Colen Campbell publishes *Vitruvius Britannicus* 1722 James Gibbs designs St Martin-in-the-Fields James 'Athenian' Stuart introduces Greek style 1755 Founding of Venetian Academy, Tiepolo 1st President 1760 Thomas Jefferson builds Monticello 1762 Death of Beau Nash 1762 Josiah Wedgwood appointed Queen's Potter 1762-1771 Walpole's *Anecdotes of Painting in England* 1768 Founding of Royal Academy, Reynolds 1st President Picturesque style in garden design 'Capability' Brown landscapes gardens at Blenheim, Petworth etc 1787 *The Botanical Magazine*	Samplers become squarer and scattered with small motifs, verses, etc within frame of trailing flowers 'Hollie Point', darning and map samplers 1727 Chinoiserie tapestries woven at Soho factory Large scale canvas work, hangings, screens, etc Crewel work invaded by refined naturalistic flowers and used for dresses, jackets, shoes, etc Embroidered aprons Much decorative quilting on petticoats and as background to carefully shaded silk flowers on bed coverlets, etc Florentine stitch popular Embroidered dresses, waistcoats, etc Fine white work on muslin dresses, aprons, etc often in chain stitch worked with tambour hook Vogue for patchwork and 'drizzling' 1770 Invention of the Spinning Jenny 1770-1790 Goya designs cartoons for tapestry Needle paintings of Mary Linwood Decline in standard of technique towards end of century *c* 1780 Machine for making net invented 1789 First power-driven loom Medieval tapestries burnt during French Revolution
Buildings: Balmoral, Sandringham, Crystal Palace, Royal Exchange, Library of Lincoln's Inn, Paris Opera House, Eiffel Tower, Notre Dame (Montmartre), Gothic Revival churches, Saltaire model mill town 1810 Goya's etchings *The Disasters of War* 1810-1811 Nash formulates plans for Regent's Park John Claudius Loudun develops London squares 1816 Coleridge publishes *Kublai Khan* 1820 Blake's illustrations for *The Book of Job* Letters of Fanny Burney and Mrs Delany 1833 First modern flower show 1834 Founding of Royal Institute of British Architects 1835-1860 Barry builds Houses of Parliament 1843 Ruskin publishes *Modern Painters* 1847 British Museum completed 1848 Pre-Raphaelite Brotherhood 1851 Joseph Paxton designs gardens at Chatsworth etc 1859 Darwin publishes *Origin of Species* 1861 Royal Horticultural Society's Garden, Kensington 1865-1875 Great period of French Impressionism 1867-1896 Gilbert and Sullivan operas 1871 Royal Albert Hall and Albert Memorial 1874 Opening of St Pancras Station 1887 Arts and Crafts Exhibition, London Jane Loudon publishes books on gardening for women Mrs Beeton's recipe book, etc 1900 Art Nouveau Exhibition, Paris	*c* 1804 First canvas work patterns in colour on point paper issued in Berlin 1809 Invention of bobbin net Introduction of Berlin (Zephyr) wools and double canvas Craze for Berlin work on chairs, footstools, hand screens, bell pulls, slippers, etc Combination of beads, wool and canvas popular By 1820 lace made by machine 1828 Invention of embroidery machine White work on christening robes, caps, flounces, etc, chiefly as cottage industry in Scotland and Ireland; *c* 1836 known as Ayrshire work; superceded by *broderie anglaise* and Mountmellick embroidery Quilting clubs in rural areas Patchwork popular Coarse embroidery on rural smocks 1851 Elias Howes' lockstitch machine 1854 Ladies' Ecclesiastical Embroidery Society, Leek Embroidery Society *c* 1860 Revival of interest in crewel wools 1862 Nottingham making lace by machine in imitation of Mechlin, Valenciennes, Chantilly and Brussels laces 1865 Shuttle or *schifflé* machine William Morris and the Arts and Crafts Movement Fashion for art needlework Revival of cutwork now called Richlieu work 1872 Royal School of Needlework founded

Illustration credits

Permission to reproduce the black and white photographs has kindly been given by the following (illustration numbers given).

From a privately bound edition of Stothard's drawings of the Bayeux Tapestry, 1, 4, 5, 6, 7. Crown copyright, Victoria and Albert Museum, London, 8, 22, 28, 38, 41, 43. Author's photographs, 11, 17, 18, 19, 20, 70. National Museum of Ireland, Dublin, 16. Crown copyright, British Museum, London, 21. The Board of Governors, Museum of London, 23. The National Trust, Cotehele House, Cornwall, 29. Victoria and Albert Museum, London, 30, 40, 42, 50, 53, 54, 55, 64. Museum of Fine Arts, Boston, Elizabeth Day McCormick Collection, 33. The National Trust, Wallington, Northumberland, photograph supplied by The Victoria and Albert Museum, London, 39. The National Trust, Blickling Hall, Norfolk, 44. Northampton Museum and Art Gallery, 45. Leicester Museum and Art Gallery, 56, 59. William Morris Gallery, Walthamstow, London, 65, 66, 67. George Howard Esq, on loan to the Victoria and Albert Museum, London, 71. Lady Weaver, 72. The National Trust, Wallington, Northumberland, 73. Mr and Mrs John R. Williams, 77. Dean and Chapter, Winchester Cathedral, 78, 79, 80. Williamson Art Gallery and Museum, Birkenhead, 85. Joyce Judd, 86. Mrs Judy Egerton, on page 6.

The following have taken photographs specially for this book (illustration numbers given; those in italic refer to colour).

C. Cannings, 1, 4, 5, 6, 7, *10*, *12*, *13*, *24*, *25*, 30, *31*, *32*, *34*, *35*, *36*, 40, 42, *46*, *49*, 50, *51*, *52*, 53, 54, 55, *57*, *58*, *61*, *62*, *63*, 64, *68*, *69*, 71, *75*, *76*, *81*, *82*, *83*, *84*.
R. Chapman Photography, Plymouth, 29.
A. E. Coe and Sons Ltd, Norwich, 44.
A. C. Cooper Ltd, London, 26, 27, 72, 74, 77, 86, *88*, 89, 90, 91, 92, *93*, *94*.
W. Cull Ltd, Birkenhead, 85.
E. A. Sollars, Winchester, 78, 79, 80, *87*.
Desmond Trip Studios, Bristol, *47*, *48*.
Turners Ltd, Newcastle, 73.

Index

Page numbers in italic refer to illustrations